GATHERING POWER
THROUGH INSIGHT
AND LOVE

GATHERING POWER

THROUGH INSIGHT AND LOVE

Ken Keyes, Jr.,
Penny Keyes,
and Staff

First Edition

LIVING LOVE PUBLICATIONS
Coos Bay, Oregon 97420

BOOKS BY KEN KEYES, JR.

Handbook to Higher Consciousness
How to Enjoy Your Life in Spite of It All
A Conscious Person's Guide to Relationships
Gathering Power Through Insight and Love
(with Penny Keyes and Staff)
Prescriptions for Happiness
Your Heart's Desire
Taming Your Mind
The Hundredth Monkey
How to Make Your Life Work or
Why Aren't You Happy?
(withTolly Burkan)

HELPFUL INFORMATION

TO ORDER: *Gathering Power Through Insight and Love* is available for $6.95 in bookstores or from the Ken Keyes College Bookroom, 790 Commercial Ave., Coos Bay, OR 97420. Please add $1.25 for mailing costs. You may order using VISA or MasterCard. (503) 267-4112.

TO STUDY: You can write to the Ken Keyes College for information on nonprofit personal growth workshops and courses ranging from a weekend to several months. You will receive a free catalog listing other personal growth books, audiotapes, and videotapes on the Science of Happiness. Write to Ken Keyes College, 790 Commercial Avenue, Coos Bay, Oregon 97420, or phone (503) 267-6412.

TO QUOTE: The Twelve Pathways, drawings, or portions of this book not exceeding a total of 1000 words may be freely quoted or reprinted without permission provided credit is given in the following form: Reprinted from *Gathering Power Through Insight and Love* by Ken Keyes, Jr., Penny Keyes, and Staff. Copyright 1987 by Living Love Publications.

LIBRARY OF CONGRESS CATALOGING-IN-PUBLICATION DATA:
Keyes, Ken.
Gathering power through insight and love.
   1. Success. 2. Love. 3. Conduct of life.
I. Keyes, Penny. II. Title.
BJ1611.2.K49 1987   158'.1   86-20913
ISBN 0-915972-11-5 (pbk.)

First Printing, December 1986   10,000
Second Printing, January 1987   <u>10,000</u>
Total: 20,000

DEDICATION

**This book is dedicated to all the
past, present, and future students of
Living Love through whom
the Science of Happiness
has been brought to life.**

ACKNOWLEDGMENTS

The experience of tens of thousands of students and hundreds of staff members have contributed to the development of the life-enriching skills in this book. It has evolved from *The Methods Work...If You Do!* produced by the residents of the Cornucopia Institute. Kris Nevius, Debbie Ham, and Carole Thompson at the Institute particularly played an outstanding part in creating the earlier version. We also acknowledge the contribution of ideas we've adapted from the work of Richard Bandler and John Grinder.

Aura Wright, a teacher at the Ken Keyes College in Coos Bay, Oregon, has added many valuable insights and suggestions to *Gathering Power Through Insight and Love*. Although Aura helped improve every chapter, her suggestions for Positive Intentions, Consciousness Focusing, core beliefs, and the SOS were invaluable. Tom Kornbluh also offered valuable ideas. Ann Hauser typed the entire book and all revisions, prepared camera-ready copy, and contributed many excellent suggestions to improve the text. Bill Hannig assisted with the typographical design and Coni Fritz with editing.

Without the wonderful creative energy of these and many other individuals too numerous to mention, this book would not be available.

Ken and Penny Keyes
Coos Bay, Oregon
December 1986

LOVE IS THE ANSWER

Hate begets hate,
violence engenders violence,
hypocrisy is answered by hypocrisy,
war generates war,
and love creates love.

Dr. Pitirim A. Sorokin
Department of Sociology
Harvard University

When things are bad, say they are bad;
but don't hate the ones who do those things.

Archbishop Desmond Tutu
Nobel Peace Prize Winner

If you want to see the brave,
look at those who can forgive.
If you want to see the heroic,
look at those who can love
in return for hatred.

Mahatma Ghandi
Political Leader

True [unconditional] love is unconquerable and
irresistible and goes on gathering power and
spreading itself, until eventually it transforms
everyone whom it touches. Humanity will attain to
a new mode of being through the free and
unhampered interplay of pure love from heart to
heart.

Meher Baba
Indian Philosopher

...love your enemies, bless those who curse you,
do good to those who hate you....

Christ at the
Sermon on the Mount

CONTENTS

INTRODUCTION

Published in 1972, the *Handbook to Higher Consciousness* has over three quarter million copies in print. Many bookstores have reported that customers sometimes buy out the entire stock to give to their friends. *Gathering Power Through Insight and Love* was written to help you get these life-enriching ideas even more effectively into your daily life—including your interactions with other people. We view our life work as living and teaching a "Science of Happiness"—tools to forge a happy life.

The Science of Happiness has four parts:

1. **BODY:** Holistic support of the body-mind complex through exercise, modern nutrition, and a knowledge of your individual biochemical responses to environmental substances. This aspect is not discussed in *Gathering Power Through Insight and Love*. For this information we currently recommend *The Aerobics Program for Total Well-Being*, revised edition, by Kenneth Cooper, M.D.; *Eat to Succeed* by Dr. Robert Haas; *Brain Allergies: The Psychonutrient Connection* by William H. Philpott, M.D. and Dwight K. Kalita, Ph.D. (with an introduction by Linus Pauling, Ph.D.); and *An Alternative Approach to Allergies* by Theron G. Randolph, M.D. and Ralph W. Moss, Ph.D. (a revolutionary individualized program for eliminating environmental illnesses and brain malfunctions through the new science of clinical ecology).

2. **MIND:** Techniques for teaching the rational mind (left brain) to make decisions that yield the results we want. This part of the Science of Happiness is presented in *Taming Your Mind* by Ken Keyes, Jr. and is not discussed in this book.

3. **LIVING LOVE:** Skill in freeing our loving spirit so that we can create a world of love around us—both inside us and in the hearts of those around us. *Gathering Power Through Insight and Love* can help people develop this skill that is essential to an effective, fulfilling, joyous, peaceful, and loving life.

4. HELPING OTHERS: The final touchstone of the Science of Happiness includes a recognition that our own lives are enriched to the degree that we
enrich the lives of others. *We mean this literally.* It is through loving and
serving other people and the world around us that we are freed from the
continuous preoccupation and worry of the separate-self. This opens the
door to progressively enjoying the fulfilling experience of the unified-self.
For more guidelines in this part of the Science of Happiness, we suggest
How Can I Help? by Ram Dass and Paul Gorman.

There are many paths that one can use on the journey of personal growth.
Although many of them appear to be unique, the authors think that most ways
of personal growth, in their essence, are remarkably similar. We wish to present
our particular version that we call the "Science of Happiness" for your consideration. It is not for everyone; each of us must explore and choose the personal
growth path that most liberates the energies of his or her own body, mind, and
loving spirit.

HOW TO GET THE MOST FROM THIS BOOK

The authors are not aware of any quick fixes that can permanently wipe out
the fears, frustrations, desperations, disappointments, and alienations experienced in a human life. But we do know that we personally, as well as countless
others, have gradually experienced lasting new dimensions of enjoyable living
using these Science of Happiness techniques. And the benefits continue to
increase geometrically as we develop our mastery of these skills. We view personal growth as a lifetime journey.

The Science of Happiness is not a belief system. Like a saw, you don't have to
believe it works—it does the job if you just use it. The results improve with
practice.

As an aid to the mastery of the life-giving Science of Happiness, we have
organized this book into **two Wisdom Principles, four Living Love Methods,
and four Dynamic Processes—the "2-4-4 system."** These principles, methods,
and processes are designed to be used on the spot in daily life. For instance, all
of them can be used in a crowded elevator if someone yells "Fire!" Like all good
methods, they work if you do.

This book is for you to read and reread. Intellectually absorbing its contents
will probably give you some new approaches for perceiving people and situations. And we hope that will happen the way you want. Yet our main emphasis

lies in presenting **action techniques.** The last chapter is titled *Action Summary!* If you really want to gather the power of insight and love within yourself, you must do your part to develop your skill. *Use the 2-4-4 techniques.* After reading it through, review little bits of the book thoughtfully from time to time. Imagine being comfortable with the concepts and procedures.

> **THE 2-4-4 SYSTEM**
> *2 Wisdom Principles*
> *4 Living Love Methods*
> *4 Dynamic Processes*

Experiment and practice with them so that, as your skill increases, you can use them automatically when you feel uncomfortable or unhappy. Accept the challenge to begin the transition from generating your experience out of your *separate-self* to creating it with your *unified-self*. We bet that with such application, qualitative changes will begin that will dramatically enhance your life.

You can enjoy your journey of continuing personal growth. That's what it's all about! You can appreciate and love *yourself* and your life as you increasingly use the Science of Happiness to gain insight and inner peace. About half of our marriages are ending in divorce; our world could be blown up through fear, frustration, and hatred among nations. Ways of increasing our understanding and cooperation are vitally needed for both *individual happiness and human survival.* We invite you to increasingly add the empowering energy of insight and love to your own life—and to our planet! You can start right now.

> **EMPOWER YOURSELF THROUGH UNCONDITIONAL LOVE!**

Part 1

TWO
WISDOM
PRINCIPLES

1 WHAT DO YOU WANT FROM YOUR LIFE?

♥ *We all want to feel good about our lives—to feel that we're getting what's gettable—to live satisfying and fulfilling lives. Have our parents, our schools, the TV, or our friends shown us how to do this?*

♥ *What are the ways in which we destroy our energy, our insight, and our ability to appreciate and love other people and ourselves?*

♥ *What are the techniques that can help us live enjoyable and effective lives?*

THE SEPARATE-SELF

There's no doubt about it. We all want what we want when we want it. The difference between an enjoyable, loving life and a self-centered, blaming, unhappy life lies more in how we go about getting what we want—and our psychological response when we don't get it. It is the same for all of us: *we win some and we lose some.* The key to identifying a person who has the enormous power of love working for him/her is to notice (1) how the person goes about trying to win and (2) how s/he responds when s/he loses one of the games of life.*

Let's look at how people who feel ineffective, unloving, and unhappy thrash about trying to get what they want in life. They feed their energy through what we will call the "separate-self." The separate-self automatically casts each situation into a "me-vs.-them" framework which creates life as serious, threatening, stressful, and combative. People living through the separate-self will experience life as a battle against other people, the world—or even themselves. Some of the most devastating ravages of the separate-self habits of mind are *me vs. my mind,*

---

* "S/he" is to be read as "she or he."

3

me vs. my personality, and *me vs. my body*. In these *me-vs.-me* and *me-vs.-you* wars, these folks try all kinds of strategies. Many of them work to a limited extent. And none of them consistently yields enjoyment, happiness, appreciation, or love of oneself and other people. The joy of living is missing.

What are the limited separate-self ways people use to try to get what they want? At various times they run away from situations they don't like, blame and criticize themselves or others, cleverly try to manipulate and control people by being quick to anger, instantly withdraw affection and love when they dislike something, become physically violent, become intellectually judgmental—and often combinations of these. They may be respected or feared and their lives often may seem to work fairly well on the outside. *However, fear chases away the experience of love inside, and they live isolated, separate, and lonely lives inside even when surrounded by friends or family.*

The separate-self *me vs. you* prompts people to misunderstand us, suspect us, mistrust us, and fight us. It destroys our marriages, our enjoyment of ourselves and our family, and in the international scene may result in our blowing up the world.

This book is for those of us who are eager to go beyond the separate-self ways to get what we want from our lives. We've all tried them and they just don't work that well. Although they can yield some satisfaction, they let us down in the end. Our *me-vs.-you* mental habits keep us locked into creating hollow lives. Outwardly we may appear fine to others, but inside each of us knows where the shoe pinches.

THE UNIFIED-SELF

There is an ancient story of an argument between the sun and the wind about who was the more powerful. A man happened to be walking by. The sun and the wind agreed to a contest to find out who could get the man to remove his coat. The wind went first. His opening blast almost stripped the coat away. He blew and he howled, and he sent one powerful gust after another to rip the coat off the man. It was a real *me-vs.-you* battle between the wind and the man to blow his coat away. And the stronger the wind blew, the tighter the man pulled his coat around him. Finally the wind gave up.

Then it was the sun's turn. The sun came out from behind a cloud and warmly greeted the man in his generous way. There was no separate-self, *me vs. you*, or "I'll force you to do what I want." Instead the sun used the unified-self approach of *me and you*. The man was getting warmer and soon he unbuttoned

4

his coat as he walked along. The sun continued to radiate as usual. After a few minutes the man decided to remove his coat and carry it. With its *me-and-you* approach, the sun had prevailed over the wind who used a separate-self *me-vs.-you* way of getting what it wanted.

The power we gather through insight and love is not a dominating type of power. Consider instead a new model of power—one that does not involve the *me-vs.-you* pattern of brute force we inherited from the jungle. This is an empowerment that comes from within us based on our insight and love. (The word *power* is derived from the Old French *poeir*—to be able.) This more effective type of power is based on our ability to work with situations and people. It's cooperative power rather than dictatorial power.

DEFINITIONS

SEPARATE-SELF: *The mental programs that create the experience of your life as a battle against yourself, other people, and the world. The illusory "me-vs.-you" perceptions that guard your addictive demands.*

UNIFIED-SELF: *The mental programs that create a compassionate, understanding, and wise insight into people and situations. The "me-and-you" programming that gives you an overall perspective of how everything fits perfectly into your journey through life, either for your growth or your enjoyment.*

It is based on understanding, caring, win-win solutions, love, upleveling demands to preferences, tuning-in to positive intentions in which both parties feel good about it, and above all, *flowing one's energy through the unified-self instead of the separate-self.*

This book shows us how to use the resources of our minds to see, hear, and feel the new world we can create and inhabit as we make the transition from the separate-self to the unified-self. Let's take a look at some of the highlights in this journey of personal growth. One of the first things that happens is that a great burden of self-centered worries begins to lift from our minds. Gradually we are relieved of the heavy load of guilt, self-doubt, perfectionistic models, and destructive illusions regarding ourselves and others.

We start to realize that the separate-self has kept us trapped in creating a special personally biased version of the people around us and the circumstances of our lives. Since we have usually surrounded ourselves by friends who have had similar separate-self illusions, we have often remained trapped in our particular rat race. Bit by bit we appreciate how the separate-self programming we picked up as children has kept us in a jail of our own making. We recognize that feelings of anger, hate, and fear are counterproductive energies of the separate-self. We begin to notice that what we most reject in other people is what we most reject in ourselves.

BENEFITS OF THE UNIFIED-SELF

The separate-self tries to find loving relationships; the unified-self creates loving relationships. Through the mirror effect, the unified-self radiates caring, cooperation, and helpfulness which is usually reflected back by others.

As we continue the journey from the separate-self into the unified-self response to everyday events, we increasingly realize that we don't have to endure life as a serious, cliff-hanging, stressful day-by-day grind. And instead of experiencing people as difficult or impossible to control in order to achieve the "reasonable" things that we want in our lives, our perception enters a new dimension. The game now lies more in harmonizing our energies—not in controlling other people.

The criticalness and judgmentalness of the separate-self slowly dissolves as we make it okay to be ourselves. We develop patience when things do not always happen at the time and in the way desired. We are able to create the experience of being caught in a traffic jam as a peaceful interlude instead of a stressful trap. And as people perceive that our love is becoming unconditional, they increasingly trust enough to be open and "real" with us.

Through the unified-self, we can now enjoy the abundance our lives always offer us—but which we have ignored up to now. We appreciate the cup of life as being half full—and let go of the separate-self perception that it is half empty. We savor living right now and are constantly aware that we have more than we need to feel happy and fulfilled. We come to view our lives with insight and a greater perspective as we quiet the separate-self that has been jumping up and down inside us complaining that we don't have enough to be happy.

As the clouds lift from our daily feelings, we no longer feel stressed or worried about the future. Through the clear vision of the unified-self, we see that we live in a world in which everything is a "process"—and change is synonymous with life.

We frequently watch ourselves as actors and actresses on the cosmic stage—playing our parts in the "soap opera" of our lives. Through the unified-self, we acknowledge that consciously or unconsciously we've chosen the parts we are playing. We know we have many capabilities and do not need to trap ourselves in any particular role. And we are aware that the things we say and do have consequences that will set up the next act in the drama of our lives.

We no longer judge ourselves mercilessly in a way that requires us to pay the price of losing our self-esteem and self-confidence when our "humanness" or lack of skill does not permit us to live up to our ideals. As the habits of the unified-self become more automatic, we find that we can retain high ideals without tearing ourselves apart through self-downing and self-criticism. While some situations in life need dynamic attention from us, we know that fear and hatred always keep us from finding the most harmonious and effective long-run solutions to life's challenges.

We open our eyes to the incredible situation of being a member of an endangered species with the power to self-destruct in this nuclear age. We understand that the problem has little to do with nuclear missiles; *it is created in the separate-self habits of all of us.* We come to know that these self-centered *me-vs.-you* patterns cannot enable us to be happy individuals—or to survive on this planet. **We are beginning to understand that only the transition to unified-self habits of mind can enable us to meet the challenges of this stage of our human evolution.**

YOUR GREAT POTENTIAL

The greatest adventure of your life awaits you as you make the transition into your unified-self. Your separate-self creates and inhabits a "dangerous" world. It must constantly be on guard against people who will take advantage of it. Or deceive it. Or hurt it. Or abuse it. Or steal from it, lie to it, or cheat it. Danger lurks everywhere. And the more it guards itself, *the more it attracts other separate-self energy.* **This acts as a self-fulfilling prophecy and our worst fears often prove to be justified.**

This lonely, beleaguered, and threatened life of the separate-self undergoes a miraculous metamorphosis as one creates one's thoughts and actions through the unified-self. The self-fulfilling "truth" of the separate-self *me-vs.-you* dissolves into the higher, equally self-fulfilling truth of the unified-self with its *me and you.*

The separate-self hopes for and tries to use the energy of love. The unified-self **is** the energy of love. And what is love? Love is a heart-to-heart feeling of togetherness and closeness—with few separating boundaries—*that you create and maintain in yourself.* Loving energy tends to generate a two-way cooperation, togetherness, mutual support, understanding, patience, forgiveness, compassion, peace of mind, and enjoyment of the miracle of life. You don't necessarily have to agree with people; you just don't throw them out of your heart. And love is something beyond what words can point to: a feeling of *"This is it."*

We begin to realize that a happy and fulfilling life cannot be built upon getting more and more security, delightful sensations, power, money, fame, or feeding one's pride. The problem is one of "enoughness." Our separate-self programming will never tell us that we have enough security, enough delightful sensations, enough power, enough money, enough fame, or enough of anything to create an inner serenity that feels like "Ah, now I've got enough and I can be happy."

Only when we deeply appreciate and love ourselves and others can we sustain this glowing unified-self experience. And we can be very clear that we must not demand loving thoughts and actions from other people; instead, we can trust that if we radiate love continuously, *it will be mirrored back to us in greater quantity and quality than we need to be happy.*

Through the experience of the unified-self we thus learn the master secret of human life: **LOVE IS THE ANSWER.** It is the basic foundation for a happy life. And unified-self love is always unconditional. No strings attached. I may not like what you do or say (and I may even try to change you), but my love for you remains unflickering through all the ups and downs of life. The bookkeeping type of love generated by the separate-self is not really love. It is a transaction between two people: "I'll love you as long as you love me and do what I want." This is brittle, explosive, undependable, not lasting.

The radiant love of the unified-self is like the warmth of the sun that falls upon all alike. The sun's gift is bestowed evenly without regard to who deserves it, who needs it or who will return it. *The dynamic ability to lift humanity into a transcendent new plane of fulfillment on planet earth can be achieved only by empowering ourselves through the insight and love generated by the unified-self.*

Although love is a cornerstone of all spiritual paths, very few people really hear the message that love is the most powerful energy in the universe. Love can do what nothing else can; it helps us create cooperation and support that would not otherwise exist from other people; it enables us to appreciate and understand everyone as it increasingly frees us from *me-vs.-them* battles. The stresses created by the separate-self are wearing out our bodies at a very rapid rate; scientific research has shown that love offers us one of the keys to a more healthful body and a longer life.

The unified-self enables us to appreciate our lives as humorous and adventurous games we choose to play. We're never as protected and safe as when we radiate unconditional love. For when others mirror back this love, as they will inevitably do, they automatically extend an umbrella of caring awareness that gives us the ultimate in security. As we develop the program of the unified-self with its *me-and-you* approach to life situations, we create an experience of life that is more effective in the long run, far more enjoyable, and feels less like a roller coaster between pleasure and pain.

We designed this book to assist you with the transition from separate-self skills to unified-self skills. *It shows you what to do and how to do it.* It gives you a variety of ways to choose from that help you actualize your unified-self in every life situation. This smorgasbord of techniques includes **two Wisdom Principles, four Living Love Methods, plus four Dynamic Processes.** As you master and apply the techniques of the Science of Happiness, you will begin to automatically transform your life into what you've always wanted—but perhaps haven't consistently found.

> **A JOURNEY OF A THOUSAND MILES**
> **BEGINS WITH A SINGLE STEP.**
>
> Lao Tsu

2 YOUR DEMANDS CREATE YOUR UNHAPPINESS

♥ *We've all known fear, frustration, anger, and many other uncomfortable feelings. There have been countless times in our lives when we felt unhappy—or were even suffering. We've always thought we knew what was causing it: bad luck, other people not understanding us, other people treating us meanly, blaming ourselves for our own mistakes—the list of who or what to blame is endless. And we've often thought our unhappiness was caused by things largely out of our own control. The world was "doing it" to us.*

♥ *Could it be that this is an illusion based on a common error in perception? Could it be that our happiness does not depend on "outside" people and events? Could it be that we really don't realize what caused us to create uncomfortable feelings, separateness, and unhappiness? Could it be that we create our experience through widespread but erroneous habits of mind?*

♥ *YES! All of us are the authors of our own experience of life. This chapter will show how we can, regardless of the circumstances under which we live, gradually increase our enjoyment of life. We can be the masters of our experience—even though we cannot always control the people in the world around us to fit our models and desires! The world hasn't been doing it to us—we've been doing it to ourselves through unskillful mental habits. But we're not to blame either! As we begin to use the basic principle of this chapter in our everyday lives, we start to experience ourselves and the world in an entirely different way that allows us to really enjoy our lives more.*

OUR DEMANDING MINDS

Henry David Thoreau observed that "the mass of men lead lives of quiet desperation." And some of us are not so quiet! Why is continuous happiness usually considered to be an unrealistic or unattainable state? Why are we so often triggering separating emotions of fear, frustration, anger, irritation, worry, resentment, panic, hate, impatience, anxiety, exasperation, fury, and on and on into the night? What's messing up our lives???

IT'S OUR DEMANDS! It's just demands that make our minds trigger the above emotions and keep us upset so much of the time. "I can't stand that window rattling." "The nasty bugs are eating my flowers." "I'm pissed off because Lisa forgot our date." "John makes me angry when he asks why dinner isn't ready." "Those kids! They've messed up the living room again." "I'm getting too fat." "I'll never learn to keep my bank book straight." "Brad just isn't reasonable about wanting sex so much." "Jill spends money as if it grows on trees."

THE FIRST WISDOM PRINCIPLE

Everyone is entitled to enjoy love, inner peace, and a sense of unity. Unconditional love exists in every one of us, but often our programming interrupts our experience of that love. We can compare love with the ever-present sun. The sun is always shining. At times the clouds block some of the sun's rays and we automatically say, "The sun isn't shining today," although we know it's there, shining behind the clouds. Even at midnight the sun is shining. The "world has turned around" so it appears that there is no sun! Yet, when we consider, we realize that the sun is still shining.

In much the same way, heart-to-heart love is always there in us, waiting to be felt and expressed. Often our programming "clouds" our experience of loving. And at times we literally turn our emotional world around to the point where we are certain we have lost love. But it is always there.

The Science of Happiness offers us ways to clear away the clouds, and experience appreciation and love for ourselves and others. The first empowering Wisdom Principle it gives us is:

> **ADDICTIVE DEMANDS TRIGGER SEPARATING EMOTIONS THAT CREATE YOUR UNHAPPINESS. PREFERENCES NEVER DO.**

An addiction (or an addictive demand) is a desire, expectation, or model that makes you feel upset or unhappy if it is not satisfied. We call it an "addiction"

11

because you tell yourself you must have it to be happy. You might have a demand on yourself, on another person, or on a situation. For example, "I demand that I not lose my keys," or "I demand that you be on time," or "I demand that Trevor say he agrees with me." Our minds keep running demands throughout the day—and night.

The clue to knowing when you have an addictive demand is whether you feel separating emotions, tension in your body, or churning in your mind about whatever it is you want. A demand is addictive when *you think you must have it satisfied to be happy or if you feel upset in any degree.* It comes in three strengths: thinking out, emoting out, and acting out. Take a minute now to notice demands your mind has run today....

Only addictive demands can interfere with our experience of love. This means that all our unhappiness and suffering is caused by our demanding programming—*not by life events.* When there is no addictive demand, there is no suffering. When we *prefer* things to be a certain way (instead of demand), we do not create unhappiness, fear, frustration, anger, or hate—about ourselves or anyone else. With preferential programming we can always feel the love within us.

In the past, when we were aware of worry, sadness, irritation, or other separating emotions, we felt there was something in our world (a life event) that was not happening as we thought it should. That event wasn't meeting our "model" of how it should be. So, we erroneously blamed the life condition for our unhappiness:

ERRONEOUS THINKING

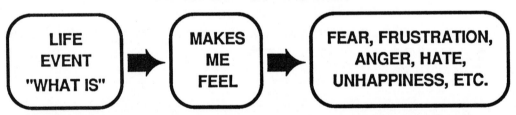

NOTE: When we use the term "life event" or "what is," we are referring to "objective reality"—the way things are unfolding in our changing world—as contrasted with the separate-self distortions in thinking and perception created in our minds. A life event (or "what is") can take place either inside us or in the world outside our skin—and is then reported to us by our various senses.

Sometimes, no matter what we do, how we act, or what we say, we can't get something to change. And there we are: the life condition won't change, and we think all we can do is to experience annoyance, resentment, anxiety, jealousy, loneliness, or some such separating emotion. This is the way we have all spent much of our lives—feeling unhappy when the outside event wasn't the way we thought it should be, and blaming ourselves or others for things not being different.

We have usually responded to our dissatisfaction by attempting to change the life event. We have put time and energy into forcing changes on ourselves and other people. We've harmed people in trying mightily to force changes. Sometimes we've gotten what we wanted, depending on how good we were at changing the world. But let's face it: *have we ever changed people and things enough for us to really enjoy our lives*—**to then peacefully live our lives?**

Let's clear up a possible misconception. There's nothing wrong with trying to change things to meet our models. We do it "all" the time. We have learned lots of ways to increase our skill in getting what we want. But what do we do when a life situation doesn't change? Feel bad? The Science of Happiness shows us what to do when our lives don't give us the changes we want—*which is usually* !

OUR PROGRAMMING CREATES OUR EXPERIENCE

The exciting opportunity the Science of Happiness offers us is the realization that we can choose to experience satisfying feelings instead of automatically triggering separating emotions. Rather than blame anyone for anything, we are learning that we can take responsibility for what we feel—and, therefore, choose the feelings we want to experience inside us—even if the outside event doesn't change.

All that's needed to change a separating emotion is to change the programming that triggers the emotion. This concept is empowering in the sense that it shows us that we have the potential to be *the masters of our own emotional experience*—any time, under any circumstance. We can't always change the life event, but with skill we can empower ourselves to change the programming that generates our *experience* of it!

The area we want to work with is our thoughts and our programming, not our actions—not even our emotions. We are careful to avoid repressing or suppressing our emotions. *Our emotions will change as we change our programming that causes them.*

Our brain has often been called a biocomputer. Just as a computer is guided by its programming, we are run by ours. We are creating our present emotions and actions from the programming we have put into our biocomputer over the years—from childhood on up!

When we acquired our programming, we may have chosen it because it worked for us at the time. However, over the years we've changed, and our situations have changed. We've developed new expectations and skills. Although outside events have changed, our programming hasn't necessarily changed with them. So today at 20, 40, or 60 years of age, we are sometimes operating from the programmings we put in when we were 2, 4, or 6 years old. And these programmings are often no longer workable to yield insight and happiness in many of our current life situations.

UPLEVELING ADDICTIONS TO PREFERENCES

In the Science of Happiness, a preference is a desire that is not triggering any separating feelings or tensions in your mind or body *whether or not your desire is satisfied*. With a preference you can dislike a situation. You can put energy into making changes with a preferential attitude, but you do not feel emotionally attached to the results—and you remain loving of yourself and others. For example, consider yourself making the statement, "I want you to be on time." The key to knowing whether a preference is operating in your mind is to notice whether you feel internally relaxed and free from any separating emotion—even when the person is not on time. Addictive demands and preferences are both wants or desires—*but are vastly different in how they affect your enjoyment*. Addictions can generate a sense of personal power when they occasionally are satisfied; preferences are the key to *continuously* powerful living!

Sometimes our ego-minds hold on to our addictive demands because we have the illusion that we need them. If I emotionally accept someone's opposing view, won't I be too wishy-washy? Won't people take advantage of me if I do not have addictions that trigger anger in at least some situations? Won't I become a doormat? If everything is a preference, won't I lose the ability to deal effectively with many situations? Won't life be boring? Won't I stop caring and trying to improve things? Won't I be trapped helplessly in hopeless situations if I uplevel all my addictive demands to preferences?

All of these questions are based on a misunderstanding of what we mean by a preference:

1. *You can still want what you want.*
2. *You can still try to make changes.*
3. *You can still think you're "right."*
4. *You can more skillfully achieve your positive intention.*
5. *You just don't have to feel upset or unhappy!*

When we operate from addictive programming, we find that when we think something happens (an "apparent life event") *which is not what we want,* we make ourselves unhappy. We often do this without understanding that it's our programming (what we are telling ourselves about this event) that causes our unhappiness. We tell ourselves *if it only were different,* then we could be happy. *What we don't realize is that it's the addictive demand programming we have about the way the event "has" to be that is making us upset—not the outside event.*

Notice the difference a preference makes even when the life event is unchanged:

HOW OUR MINDS ACTUALLY WORK

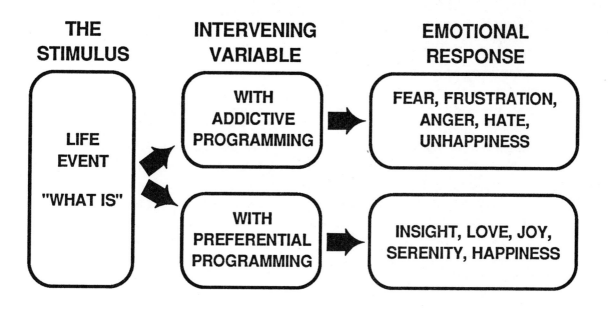

THE STIMULUS	INTERVENING VARIABLE	EMOTIONAL RESPONSE
LIFE EVENT "WHAT IS"	WITH ADDICTIVE PROGRAMMING	FEAR, FRUSTRATION, ANGER, HATE, UNHAPPINESS
	WITH PREFERENTIAL PROGRAMMING	INSIGHT, LOVE, JOY, SERENITY, HAPPINESS

15

BECOMING A CREATIVE CAUSE

We can adjust our perceptions about situations in which we feel unhappy. Increasing our awareness of two things helps us become "creative causes" instead of "victims" of life:

1. **WE CREATE OUR EXPERIENCE:** The addictive demands that we have programmed into our heads are the immediate, practical cause of our unhappiness when the world isn't the way we want it to be. In the boxes above, notice that our addictive programming immediately precedes our internal experience. Handling our addictive demands is useful because *it offers us a way to change our internal experience to a more desirable one.* For example, if a person criticizes us, this life event in itself cannot make us hurt or angry. It can only trigger an addictive programming we may have that people not criticize us. If we do not have this addictive programming, there is no way that criticism can reach into our minds and stimulate the emotional centers (limbic area) to create our experience of hurt or anger. It is instead just noticed as another event in our lives. And we then have many options in our response instead of the narrow range of options offered by our minds when we are generating fear, anger, frustration, resentment, etc. Upleveling our addictive demands to preferences enables us to be *creative causes* instead of *victims* in our various life circumstances.

2. **WE ARE NOT OUR PROGRAMMING:** In our essence, we are not our programming and we are not the thoughts and feelings generated by our preferential or addictive programming. For example, no matter how beautiful or unpleasant the music on our stereo seems to us, *the music is not the stereo set.* The music is generated by the cassette or program that we put into the stereo. If we don't like the music, we don't criticize our stereo set—we just change the program. If we don't like the experience we create (such as fear, frustration, or anger) in a given situation in our lives, we don't need to criticize ourselves because it means nothing about us. We can just change the program inside us! We are not victims; we are not unworthy; we are not helpless and life is not hopeless. *We are not our programming any more than the stereo set is the music that is coming from it.*

Just as a good stereo deserves a good cassette, we deserve every beautiful gift that life has to offer us. We have such potential for energy, insight, love, joy, and inner peace in our lives, and it's only our programming that is blocking our attaining them. So our goal becomes very clear: Let's begin to identify the programs in our minds that produce the "discordant music" of separateness and negative emotions. And let's get rid of them! Let's increase our skill in choosing programming that creates love, enjoyment, cooperation, and unity in our lives at every moment.

Our programming, **not us**, is responsible for our separating emotions; and *as adults we can take responsibility for our programming!* If we do not deal with our self-defeating tapes, we will miss our opportunities to creatively mold them in ways that yield happier lives. Unless we learn to change our programming, we'll be robots. We'll fight valiantly like Don Quixote against the arms of the windmills—constantly hurting himself under the illusion that he's defending his world against the dragons.

The 2-4-4 system shows us how to retrain our minds to change our addictive programming if we choose. It also offers us a new way to deal with our separating emotions: we no longer have to suppress them, and we no longer have to express them like robots! We can eliminate the addictive demands that trigger them. As we retrain our minds to select new programming and give new operating instructions to our biocomputer, we empower ourselves to live more loving, peaceful, and effective lives.*

MAKING YOUR LIFE WORK BETTER

We all have tried to make our lives "work." We have tried to find love, peace, and happiness by attempting to get "enough" or to be "enough": by acquiring "enough" money; by getting "enough" education; by finding the "right" job; by personal achievement and success; by attaining prestige, power, or fame; by getting a new home or car; by forcefully controlling our behavior and/or the behavior of others; by finding a companion; by engaging in sex; by vowing marriage or by having children; and on and on.

These are ways of trying to do what society taught us we "should" do to be happy. We have tried to be "good" people; we've tried to do the "right" things. Yet even when our lives seemingly have gone well, there has still been a certain hollowness—the feeling that "there must be more to life."

So the maneuvering to avoid fear, frustration, and anger and the search to find love and contentment have continued. We have problems in our

---

* You may find it particularly helpful to supplement the information in this chapter by reading Chapters 1, 2, and 3 of *How to Enjoy Your Life in Spite of It All* by Ken Keyes, Jr. Appendix A contains ordering information.

relationships and often seem to handle them ineffectively. We feel challenged by such concerns as, "What do I do when I feel afraid or angry? Retreat? Attack? Ignore?" "Won't people run over me if I don't fight back?" "Can other people really love me?" "Is it really possible to love unconditionally?" "How do I genuinely feel love in my life?"

The Science of Happiness empowers us through the loving energy of the unified-self. Love creates cooperation, energy, insight, and fun in our lives. By using the two Wisdom Principles, four Living Love Methods, and four Dynamic Processes, we can utilize times when we are feeling unhappy as opportunities to grow—opportunities to learn to *emotionally* accept what is happening in our lives. We begin to consciously choose the way we respond to "tough situations" using many options available through the unified-self.

You may be asking, "Even if it is possible, do I really want to emotionally accept everything that is happening in my life—even the things I don't like?" Once you realize that emotional acceptance frees you from unhappy feelings while it opens up choices for you that you were unaware of before, you will likely decide that emotional acceptance is all gain and no loss. Remember: *When you emotionally accept a situation or person, you can still put as much energy as you wish into trying to set up your world and yourself as you want them to be.* You can keep your opinions and still think you're right. The Science

---

IMPORTANT TERMS USED

Let's tune-in together so that the words we use to communicate will point to the same things:

ADDICTION/ADDICTIVE DEMAND: *A separate-self expectation or model that makes you feel upset or unhappy if it is not satisfied. A demand that causes mind disturbance, body tension, separating emotions, and/or a me-vs.-another action.*

PREFERENCE: *A desire that does not trigger any separating feelings or tensions in your mind or body whether or not your desire is satisfied.*

SEPARATING EMOTION: *A feeling stemming from the separate-self such as fear, frustration, or anger that creates the illusion of alienation from yourself and/or other people.*

UNHAPPINESS: *The unconscious or conscious experience of any separating feeling in any degree. When unhappiness is more or less continual, you experience suffering.*

PROGRAMMING: *A sequence of conscious or unconscious instructions set in your mind that play a part in interpreting the input of your feelings, various senses, and in guiding your thoughts and actions.*

EGO-MIND: *A compound term referring to the joint operation of the ego when it selects and implements which program to put into operation, and other parts of the mind that carry out the chosen program through mechanisms that perceive, think, interpret, remember, reason, emote, feel, etc.*

of Happiness shows you how to create a unified-self experience. Your increased insight and love can then enable you to more effectively make changes you want in your life. Yes, you can learn to experience emotional acceptance, keep your heart open, and live an effective life. You can progressively learn to

LOVE EVERYONE UNCONDITIONALLY—
INCLUDING YOURSELF!

DOING YOUR INNER WORK DILIGENTLY—GENTLY

There are many things you can do when you are experiencing separating emotions. The Science of Happiness offers lots of 2-4-4 options. One choice, of course, is not using any of them at all! You can choose to express your feelings or even suppress them—just be aware of what *that* creates in your life. Whatever you choose offers you an opportunity for growth. You can use the Living Love Methods—*or any other way*—to uplevel your addictive programming to preferential programming so you can enjoy your life more.

Honor your addictive demands. There is absolutely nothing "wrong" with addictions. All addictions are messages—they can be considered gifts. They are simply flags that are signaling, "Hey! At this point in your life, you are letting past programming interfere with your present potential for love and enjoyment!"

In order to go beyond your addictive programming, it is important that you let yourself be exactly where you are, experiencing whatever you are feeling. There's no need to pretend that you do not have separating emotions, or any addictions, or that you are "always" loving. In fact, resisting the idea that you have addictions and separating emotions will only delay you in letting go of the demands and becoming free of the separateness they cause. Breathe deeply and relax. Allow yourself to feel what you feel. That helps you recognize which addictions you need to explore in order to grow.

Your growing will also be impeded if you get down on yourself. That's adding another addiction! Let your path unfold in its own way—at its own rate. *You can learn to love and emotionally accept yourself here and now exactly as you are.* Realize that your strong emotions, separating thoughts and *me-vs.-them* actions are perfect for your growth. Observe that *in every moment you are either experiencing emotional acceptance and inner peace, or experiencing an opportunity to handle your addictions so that you can love more and demand less.* **You can win no matter what life gives you—or what you do!**

19

The author of *Desiderata* wrote, "Beyond a wholesome discipline, be gentle with yourself. You are a child of the universe, no less than the trees and the stars; you have a right to be here. And whether or not it is clear to you, no doubt the universe is unfolding as it should."

So, be gentle with yourself. You can get on with your inner work in the best way you know how and at the same time not blame yourself for having whatever limitations you think you have. You have come to this moment in your life with whatever programming you happened to have accumulated up to now. Each person has his or her own addictive programming to work through. Love yourself and honor the lessons your life gives you. *Don't use the Science of Happiness as another way to reject yourself when you forget to apply what you know.* And keep making the effort to create new patterns of responding to circumstances which you have allowed to upset you in the past.

One of the best ways we know to be gentle with yourself is to let go of the addiction that is keeping you feeling unhappy or separate in each moment. Just imagine feeling loving or peaceful or whatever you want, and move into that feeling. If you need help in doing that, the principles, methods, and processes are there. As you experiment and practice, you will begin to automatically sense which choice will work best for you at any particular time. And if one does not work on a given addictive demand, try another—and then another. Sometimes you may have to use all of them—several times. It's all part of the journey of life....

THE METHODS WORK— IF YOU DO!

3 HOW TO PINPOINT ADDICTIVE DEMANDS

♥ When we are feeling unhappy (experiencing separating emotions), we have one or more addictions at play. Many times our programming tells us that we must hang on to our addictive demand. Yet, in order to free ourselves from the unhappiness we are feeling, we must be willing to let go of our addictive demand or uplevel it to a preference.

♥ Before making this choice, we can benefit from knowing specifically what we are demanding in each situation.

♥ Pinpointing an addictive demand is a big step toward freedom from the demand. It helps us decide which we want more: (1) to hold on to our addictive demand or (2) to be free from the unhappiness caused by the demand.

THE ENEMY WITHIN

In living a good life, it is helpful to know what to avoid and what to go toward. In the area of health, we are learning to *avoid* high cholesterol and high blood pressure; we are learning to work *toward* optimal levels of vitamins and minerals. In developing our loving spirit, we are learning to *avoid* addictive demands that destroy our insight and love; we are learning to go *toward* preferences and positive intentions (explained in the next chapter) that enable us to create the joy of living.

As we discussed in the last chapter, addictive demands may be considered the immediate, practical cause of human unhappiness. Most of us haven't even been aware that we've had addictive demands; the separate-self prefers to put the blame for our fear, anger, frustration, and unhappiness on other people—or on ourselves rather than our programming.

Let's put the spotlight on how our addictive demands underhandedly tear us apart:

> Suppose you are engaged in a battle in which you have two allies and one enemy. Including yourself, that's 3-to-1 odds. Pretty good situation. **However, let's suppose that you do not recognize your allies, and instead mistake them for enemies.** And then to make matters even worse, let's suppose you don't recognize the true enemy at all. Since you don't recognize your enemy, it is hidden by your ignorance. So the enemy operates in the open—continually slashing at you and hurting you. Your response is constantly to mistake the source of the pain, and to lash back at your allies instead of the real enemy. So because of your tactical mistakes, you are creating odds of 3 to 1 against you. Your chances in such a battle are awful.
>
> And that's our predicament. Our allies in our consciousness growth are the people outside of us—and ourselves. But we often mistake them as enemies and blame "the enemy outside" or "the enemy inside" for our anger, fear, irritation, jealousy, resentment, and unhappiness. We blame other people for "doing it" to us—not realizing that in the normal course of their lives, they are only providing us with the painful "teachings" we need to work on our addictions. Or if we are self-rejectors, we blame ourselves—not realizing that we are our own best friend when we know who we really are.
>
> The greatest tragedy of this confused fog in which we try to live our lives is that we don't recognize the real enemy. For the real enemy is not the people and situations outside of us—nor is it ourselves. The real enemy is our addictive emotion-backed demands, which are the immediate, practical cause of all of our separateness, alienation, and unhappiness. Unless we carefully learn to recognize our addictive programming as the intervening variable between the outside world and our experience, it will continue to do its dirty work of cutting us up, and making us think that something else is doing it to us.*

Being able to pinpoint your addictive demands will heighten your effectiveness in doing the inner work needed to uplevel them to preferences. As you become aware of your addictive demands *as addictive demands*, you start to destroy the foundations of the separate-self that make you keep sinking into emotional pain. This chapter will help you develop your skill in pinpointing your addictive demands.

---

* Reprinted from *A Conscious Person's Guide to Relationships* by Ken Keyes, Jr., pp. 94-95, © 1979 Living Love Publications. Appendix A has ordering information.

HOW TO DO IT

This "Pinpointing Addictive Demands" form is designed to help you reinforce your willingness to take responsibility for your experience. It helps you avoid the error of blaming people and situations around you for your separating emotions. How often have you said, "You make me angry," *when it is always your own programming that is making you angry?*

As you read through the instructions on the next pages, work with something that is currently bothering you. This will help bring the written

---

PINPOINTING ADDICTIVE DEMANDS

I create the experience of

_____

(separating emotions)

because my programming demands that

_____ .

(formulate precisely what you want)

---

words into a living understanding. Just pinpointing an addictive demand and putting it in the form can significantly reduce its sting.

To pinpoint your specific addictive demand, first get in touch with what you are feeling. Scan your body for tension, pain, or other uncomfortable physical sensations. *Our bodies are excellent barometers of our emotional state.* They may be the first indication to us that something is bothering us. It is often easier from this vantage point to track down the specific emotions you are feeling. Your skill in identifying specific emotions and differentiating one from another will increase with practice.

Here is a list of some separating emotions you can consider when filling in the first part of the "Pinpointing Addictive Demands" form. Tune-in to your gut level feelings so that you become deeply aware (perhaps for the first time) of how you are feeling. You may be feeling one emotion or any number. Don't put down vague terms such as "unhappiness" or "separateness." Avoid using analytical descriptions such as "indecisiveness" or "slowness." To repeat: identify any and all gut level feelings, for they are the guide dogs that help you sniff out your addictive demands.

SEPARATING EMOTIONS
(Gut Level Feelings)

SECURITY TYPE: *Fear, apprehension, worry, dread, nervousness, anxiety, panic, terror, horror, despair, hurt, sadness, helplessness, grief, loneliness, shame, guilt, confusion, embarrassment, jealousy.*

SENSATION TYPE: *Frustration, grief, disappointment, boredom, disgust, jealousy.*

POWER TYPE: *Anger, resentment, annoyance, irritation, hate, frustration, jealousy, hostility, indignation, rage, impatience, disdain, exasperation, fury.*

When you are in touch with your specific emotions, listen to what your programming is telling you that you must have to be happy. There may be more than one thing that you want to be different. Sort through your demands until you come to the one central demand that you want satisfied in a particular situation and which is causing those particular emotions.

Here are questions you can ask yourself to help pinpoint what you are addictively demanding:

What do I really want in this situation?   *What would I ask a magic genie for?*
What don't I want?   *How do I think things should be?*
What do I want the most?   *How do I want myself to be?*
What do I feel I need to be happy?   *How do I think things shouldn't be?*
What would I like to be different?   *How should I be treated?*
How do I want things to be?   *What am I avoiding?*
What's bothering me the most?   *What is the threat in this situation?*
What would I complain about to my   *What's the worst thing that could*
    best friend?   *happen?*

In the precise moment you triggered the separating emotions, what did you want to change? Who did you feel separate from? When another person is involved, use his/her name. Don't be surprised if you find that your specific demands are petty, irrational, or indefensible. This is only your programming; it is not who you really are. Allow yourself to be aware of the full range of programming you have accumulated since childhood. Limiting yourself to the acknowledgment of only "good," "adult," or "socially acceptable" demands will only block you in your growth. Addictive demands are not right or wrong, fair or unfair, good or bad, sensible or silly, logical or illogical. Your addiction is simply what you emotionally want in any particular situation. Stay tuned-in to what you really feel. Be honest about what you want. Be specific, and avoid rationalizing away your addictive demands. You are lovable just the way you are—even with addictive programming.

BE MORE SPECIFIC!—THE CHALLENGE

Avoid broad, general demands such as, "I want to be happy," "I want to be loved," "I want to be treated fairly." *Be specific!* Winning the game of upleveling addictive demands to preferences means stating demands so specifically that the ego and rational mind will relax and choose to cooperate with you when you're wanting to let go of separateness. When your demands are very general, such as "I create the experience of worry and frustration because my programming demands that people like me," the demand is **SO BIG** it may have hundreds of more specific demands inside of it. Some of these might be:

> *I create the experience of anxiety and worry because my programming*
> *demands that Sam and Jane say they like my new haircut.*
> *I create the experience of loneliness and frustration because my*
> *programming demands that Bob return my phone call.*
> *I create the experience of disappointment because my programming*
> *demands that Denise ask me to go to the concert.*
> *And many, many more.*

It's easy to get impatient and want to reprogram whole general areas of addictions at once. However, a "territory" of general demands is too great for the ego and rational mind to be willing to let go of all those demands—perhaps dozens—all at the same time. So "pinpoint" your specific demands to win in the game of upleveling addictions to preferences. You may need to hunt hard. Keep trying on possible demands. The search is part of the game.

What incident triggered the separateness? In your demand, state the words you heard or wanted to hear that you used to trigger the demand. Name names. *What sensory-based observation would convince you that you got what you wanted?* Formulate your *specific* demand so precisely that you can tell whether it is being met by using your eyes or ears—instead of thinking or analyzing with your mind.

You want to make it as easy as possible for your ego-mind to accept whatever new programming you choose. Working on one specific demand at a time is the optimal way to achieve that. It's also the quickest way to reprogram your general addictive areas.

Consider a platform that is supported by many legs. The platform is a general addictive domain, and the legs are the specific demands supporting the general area. If you try to knock the platform over by jumping up and down on top of it, you won't have much success. The platform is too solid. *But by working on the specific legs, knocking them out one at a time,*

NOTICE THE DIFFERENCE

GENERAL DEMAND: *I create the experience of fear because my programming demands love.*

SPECIFIC DEMAND: *I create the experience of fear because my programming demands that Mary smile and say, "I love you."*

GENERAL DEMAND: *I create the experience of irritation because my programming demands that he not be so stupid.*

SPECIFIC DEMAND: *I create the experience of irritation because my programming demands that Bill remember his wallet when we go to the store.*

---

you reach the point where the platform is first shaky and then falls. There are simply not enough pillars left to support the platform.

It works the same way with your addictions. Once you have reprogrammed your specific demand, the insight you gain can then expand to include other addictions in that area of your programming. Your automatic emotional reactions become less intense or even nonexistent. You can let go of each similar addiction faster and faster. Your general demand can be upleveled to a preference because the individual specific demands that supported it have been reprogrammed or upleveled.

If you are still having trouble connecting with a specific demand, you can use the Exploration-Insight Process as a tool to help you explore your programming (explained in Chapter 14). If you just can't seem to pinpoint your demand, that's OK too. Even if you don't know exactly what you're addictively demanding, you can still use one or more Living Love Methods. Two of the methods are effective even if you haven't pinpointed your demand. These are the Twelve Pathways and the Centers of Consciousness, which are described in Chapters 6 and 7.

**A KEY TO LOVE AND HAPPINESS
IS NOW IN YOUR POCKET.**

**DEVELOP YOUR SKILL
IN USING IT!**

---

4 YOUR POSITIVE INTENTIONS

♥ *Are all people basically good? Are separating or evil deeds only unskillful attempts of an individual to feel good or fulfilled?*

♥ *Since we all want to be happy, could our problem be a lack of insight or skill in saying and doing that which will really make us happy?*

♥ *How can we use our addictive demands to lead us to our beneficial positive intentions? How can the understanding of our positive intentions help us deepen our appreciation and love for ourselves and others—no matter how much we may "mess up" in certain situations in our lives?*

THE SECOND WISDOM PRINCIPLE

Here is the second Wisdom Principle in the Science of Happiness:

> **BEHIND ALL OF OUR THOUGHTS, FEELINGS, AND ACTIONS, WE ALWAYS HAVE BENEFICIAL POSITIVE INTENTIONS (EVEN THOUGH WE MAY SOMETIMES USE UNSKILLFUL WAYS TO ACHIEVE THEM).**

With everyone and everything we relate to, we have a beneficial positive intention: essentially to love and/or feel loved. In many situations in our lives, we trigger addictive demands. *Behind every addiction there lies a beneficial positive intention!*

In a sense, addictive demands and positive intentions represent two sides of the same coin. Addictive demands help you spot what's causing the trouble, and positive intentions enable you to cut through directly to get what you really want. When you fully understand both of these concepts and can effectively apply them to your everyday stream of consciousness, your experience of life will go into a new dimension. The "world" will appear to change, for after all, *the world you experience is the mirror of your mind!*

As the second Wisdom Principle states, behind every thought and action lies a beneficial positive intention. At first this statement may seem outrageous. It's definitely not what we've been taught. One might say, "What about Hitler? Terrorists?

> **DEFINITION**
> POSITIVE INTENTION: *The internal experience you really want in a particular situation behind the surface demand or desire.*

The murderers and rapists? Surely their acts don't represent beneficial positive intentions!" But notice, we didn't say their acts represent beneficial positive intentions. *Behind their acts* they're always motivated by beneficial positive intentions just like yours—to feel secure, to feel effective, to feel approved of, loved, capable, happy, etc. **What they need are more skillful ways to achieve their beneficial positive intentions.** They're trapped in separate-self ways that don't work. All of this will become clearer as you read this chapter and begin to use the concept of beneficial positive intentions in your own life.

FORMULATING YOUR POSITIVE INTENTION

In the Science of Happiness, your positive intention is the *internal experience* that you really want in a particular situation underneath the surface desire. **It is basically an image, thought, or feeling you want to have.** Formulating your positive intention is simple. There are only two things you need to do. Here are the two guidelines we use for effectively uncovering beneficial positive intentions:

1. **MAKE IT BENEFICIAL AND POSITIVE:** State what you want—not what you don't want. For example, say, "My positive intention is to feel happy," rather than, "My positive intention is to not feel sad."

2. **MAKE IT IDENTIFY A DESIRED INTERNAL STATE:** Refer to a sensory-based experience or feeling in one of these three sensory modes:

   VISUAL MODE: "How do I want to see myself?" Your answer could be, "I want to see myself as humorous," or strong, wise, happy, etc.

   AUDITORY MODE: "What do I want to hear inside?" You might answer, "I want to hear inside that I'm wonderful," or beautiful, capable, winning, loved, etc.

FEELING MODE: "How do I want to feel?" Your answer might be, "I want to feel energized," or accepted, relaxed, etc.

You'll notice that there are three sensory-based modes you can choose from, depending on which you access most easily: visual, auditory, or feeling. Choose **one** mode to fill in the "Formulating Positive Intentions" form on the right.

Let's apply the two guidelines for formulating your positive intentions. You would avoid "My positive intention is to get a new house," for this does not describe an internal experience you want. And it could lock you into house hunting. Why do you want a new house? What *internal experience* do you think the house will give you? If you find that your underlying beneficial positive intention is to feel comfortable, you may discover some alternatives that can help you achieve this intention more directly than house hunting (or in addition to house hunting).

The above criteria for formulating your positive intention would also rule out "My positive intention is not to have a crowded house." Tell what you want—not what you don't want. Instead, you could formulate, "My positive intention is to feel comfortable."

The box at the right has a list of possible positive intentions that meet the criteria used in the Science of Happiness. As you can see, each one refers to an *internal experience*. *Since it is inside you, as your skill develops your emotional experience can be increasingly under your control.* Your happiness will be less and less like a

POSSIBLE POSITIVE INTENTIONS

acceptable	intelligent
accepted	joyful
accepting	knowledgeable
acknowledged	lovable
alive	loved
appreciated	loving
attractive	nurtured
beautiful	nurturing
calm	peaceful
capable	prosperous
comfortable	relaxed
competent	reliable
complete	responsible
confident	responsive
dependable	safe
energetic	satisfied
enthusiastic	secure
excited	sexual
fulfilled	sexy
fun-loving	strong
genuine	supported
happy	supportive
healthy	valuable
helpful	valued
humorous	worthwhile
important	worthy
independent	and hundreds more!

weathercock that keeps whirling around as the winds of life change. **You will gradually realize that you are your own creative cause instead of an effect of other people's behavior.** This list is not complete, so feel free to add to it in ways that reflect your own interests.

GOOD INTENTIONS BEHIND HARMFUL ACTIONS

In exploring your mind for its positive intentions, you may need to ask yourself, "What is my positive beneficial intention behind a negative, harmful thought?" Keep in mind that there are always beneficial positive intentions behind every thought or action. Even when you do things that you later regret or that others condemn, you still are motivated by beneficial positive intentions. The problem is that you may need *more skillful ways* to achieve your positive intention.

Suppose a friend has told a lie about you in order to take a business contract away from you. Let's say your thought right now is that you want to beat him up and knock his teeth in. This clearly is a negative, harmful idea. Now ask yourself, "What is my intention **behind** this harmful thought?" Perhaps your mind says, "I want to pay him back." This still does not seem like a positive beneficial intention, and it certainly doesn't point to a desired internal state. So ask yourself again, "What is my intention behind *this* idea?" Exploring inside, you might answer, "It's to feel peaceful." *So now we find that inner peace is your positive beneficial intention.* Is beating your friend up a good way to achieve this positive intention? Obviously not. At this point you can ask your mind to provide you with *new ways* to help you successfully achieve your positive intention to feel peaceful.

Begin to notice the positive intentions behind everything people do. For example, a person who robs a bank has beneficial positive intentions—one of them may be to feel (financially) secure. Don't you have this same positive intention? A difference between you and the robber is that you have more skillful ways to achieve your beneficial positive intention to feel secure. *The problem is not "bad" people—it's unskillful programming.* Think of the worst murderer you've heard of. Look over the list of "Possible Positive Intentions" and observe how many might apply to the person you're thinking about. *We can thus love everyone unconditionally and simultaneously dislike (or even try to block) the unskillful ways they are programmed to use in achieving their positive intentions!*

RECOGNIZING YOUR POSITIVE INTENTION

Experiencing separateness while trying to get your addiction met indicates an unskillful attempt to achieve your positive intention. Let's say your programming addictively demands that your partner want to go to the movies with you tonight, and because of that addiction you feel angry when s/he doesn't want to go. Behind that addiction, perhaps what you really want—your positive intention—is to feel close to that person! *The addictive demand is actually keeping you from achieving your positive intention.* In this way addictions are unskillful; they offer poor results.

When you have an addiction, here are some questions you can ask yourself to help you find your positive intention:

> *What emotions do I think I could experience by getting what I want?*
> *If I got my demand fulfilled or satisfied, how would I be feeling?*
> *What feeling am I really after by demanding that?*
> *What image of myself am I looking for behind that addiction?*
> *What thought am I hoping to hear inside if I get my demand satisfied?*

Review the two guidelines for formulating your positive intention. Follow them precisely. Here's a sample of the kind of internal dialogue that can help you sort out your positive intention:

> *I create the experience of dismay and worry because my programming*
> *   demands that I not spill coffee on the white tablecloth.*
> *What feeling are you really after by demanding that?*
> *I wouldn't think I'm clumsy.*
> *That's the feeling you don't want. What is the feeling that you do want?*
> *I want to feel acceptable. My positive intention is to feel acceptable.*

Here's another example of an internal dialogue to discover your positive intention:

> *I create the experience of hurt because my programming demands that*
> *   Tricia invite me to dinner tonight.*
> *My positive intention is that Tricia not reject me.*
> *State it in the positive: What you want instead of what you don't want.*
> *My positive intention is for Tricia to love me.*
> *That's not your internal state. What image of yourself, internal thought,*
> *   or feeling do you want?*
> *My positive intention is to hear inside that I'm lovable.*

31

Bringing together the addictive demand and positive intention helps you recognize more clearly the unskillfulness of your usual attempts at happiness. It also helps you focus on what you most want. Here are three examples of how they can be brought together:

> *I create the experience of frustration, anger, resentment, and disappointment because my programming demands that Judy clean up her room. My positive intention is to feel satisfied.*

> *I create the experience of hurt because my programming demands that Steve say I look good in my new dress. My positive intention is to see myself as attractive.*

> *I create the experience of frustration because my programming demands that Hillary kiss me more firmly and longer. My positive intention is to hear inside that I'm loved.*

Identifying your positive intention helps to open up alternative ways to achieve that intention. It helps you get out of a rut. It reminds you to love yourself with that addiction. You can perceive how your addictions are just ineffective, unskillful attempts to achieve what you *really* want behind the demand. Once you have identified the positive intention, you can approach it directly!

Remember that *your positive intentions represent what you want your life to be about.* The only thing that stops you from experiencing these 100% of the time is your lack of skill in achieving your positive intentions. Your addictive demands (often conscious) and/or your core beliefs (often unconscious) may get in the way and block you. Help is on the way! You are learning about the Wisdom Principles, the Living Love Methods, and the Dynamic Processes that can enable you to powerfully break through all of the internal roadblocks in your life.

DEVELOPING YOUR SKILL

Here is some additional information to help you tune-in to your beneficial positive intentions:

GET IN TOUCH: Be open to any possible positive intentions you may have. Frequently there may be more than one. One of the best ways to search out your deeply underlying motives which we call positive intentions is to think of a few times in your life when you were experiencing everything you wanted. Pick one of those times and ask yourself, "How did I feel?" The answer is likely to be something like, "I felt fulfilled, energized, loving, relaxed, capable." You can also ask yourself, "How did I see myself?" or "What did I hear inside about myself?" You may wish to close your eyes and do this right now.

GO FOR THEM: Tell your ego-mind not to badger you regarding the beneficial positive intentions you declare. For example, if your positive intention is "to see myself as beautiful," don't worry about whether other people see you as beautiful or not. Two purposes of formulating a positive intention are (1) to tune you in to what you really want inside, and (2) to offer you insights on addictive demands and issues in which your mind may be keeping you trapped. So do not confuse this process of *discovering your underlying motivations* by concerning yourself with what others think or with what's "real" or "true." (You can play that game some other time!) If you find yourself worried about whether others would agree or not, you've got an addiction that needs tending to. Once you've handled that, you can get back to the matter at hand—specifying the internal experience you really want for yourself.

SEPARATE POSITIVE INTENTIONS FROM GOALS: In the Science of Happiness, we distinguish between "goals" and "positive intentions." The word "goal" is used to point toward achievements we want and things we want to do. Your "goals" or "objectives" are usually your addictive demands or your preferences.

Let's compare a couple of examples: "I want to be a doctor." That's a goal. By achieving my goal, how would I feel? "I want to feel helpful." That's a positive intention. "I want to be wealthy"—goal. How would I see myself if I were wealthy? "I want to see myself as secure"—positive intention. Goals tend to be photographable and often can be perceived by other people through sight or sound; positive intentions generally are not photographable since they are internal experiences.

You will note that your *goals* may or may not be stated in the positive. For instance, you might have a goal to have no more flat tires on your car, or to avoid constipation. Behind wanting no more flat tires might be a positive intention to hear inside that you are effective, or to feel safe. If your goal is to avoid constipation, the beneficial positive intention behind it may be to see yourself as healthy, or to feel energetic.

Your addictions or goals may represent *skillful or unskillful* ways to create the feelings, images, or thoughts of your positive intentions. You can walk into a lot of unhappiness *by holding on to goals addictively.* Let your positive intentions guide you through the addictive swamps. What good things might happen if the people in the following examples let go of their addictive goals? A goal of the generals in the Pentagon is to maintain lots of nuclear missiles; one of their beneficial positive intentions may be to see themselves as protective. Sam's goal is to punish his child so severely that the child will "never lie again"; his beneficial positive intention is to feel competent. Jane's goal is to buy a mink coat; her beneficial positive intention is to hear herself say inside, "I am successful and worthwhile."

AN "INSTANT CONSCIOUSNESS DOUBLER"

Probably one of the most prevalent maladies on our planet today is our persistent habit of addictively judging one another and ourselves. This tends to keep us in a paranoid state of *person vs. person* in family life and *nation vs. nation*, pointing devastating nuclear weapons at each other. The healing of this *me-vs.-you* attitude must come from inside ourselves—where the separateness started to begin with! We will not be able to make wise decisions unless we can begin healing separate-self attitudes toward our fellow human beings and ourselves.

You can use the Positive Intention Wisdom Principle as an "Instant Consciousness Doubler" (ICD). This technique works with your family, your friends, your co-workers—all your relationships. It also works with "strangers," with groups of people, and between nations. It works when you are creating judgmentalness and separateness even from yourself. It offers you a simple process that can bring you back into a state of understanding, insight, emotional acceptance, and unconditional love—*even when you are actively working to change what is being said or done!*

USING THE ICD WHEN YOU FEEL SEPARATE FROM OTHER PEOPLE:

1. **TUNE-IN TO HIS/HER POSITIVE INTENTION:** A powerful way to get back into a loving space with someone from whom you feel separate is to find that person's positive intention. No matter how separating or despicable the actions of another person may seem to you, behind it is a positive intention. Even if it is difficult for you to figure out what that person's positive intention is, you can know that one is there—somewhere. That person simply may not have the necessary skill to bring about his/her positive

intention in a workable, unifying way. If that isn't enough for you to expand your love and compassion, put yourself in that person's shoes and imagine how it would feel to be doing or saying the same things. This may help you to understand that if you had the same programming, perhaps coming from the same life experiences, you could be acting in the same way. If you were doing the same things, what would be your positive intention behind this behavior? Would you simply be trying in an unskillful way to feel loved and secure? Knowing that people always have a beneficial positive intention that ultimately generates all of their thoughts and actions can help you increase your emotional acceptance of that person.

2. **REMEMBER IT'S ONLY PROGRAMMING:** When you feel separate from another person (or group or nation), remember that it is *your programming* that doesn't like *his/her programming*. Suppose Ralph says, "You're crazy." Use the ICD to remember it is not his essential being that you feel separate from; it's the things he is saying that you don't like. With this awareness, your love and compassion for that person can be "instantly doubled" because you are distinguishing him from his programming. He is not his programming; he is simply a fellow human being doing his best with the programming he happens to have at this time. You don't have to agree with or like his programming, and you can do all that you can to change the situation. You may even choose to have less involvement. *You just don't throw him out of your heart.*

USING THE ICD WHEN YOU FEEL SEPARATE FROM YOURSELF:

1. **TUNE-IN TO YOUR POSITIVE INTENTION:** A way to love, accept, and forgive yourself is to consider your positive intention. Know that you always have a positive intention no matter what you are doing or saying. You may simply have been unskillful at that moment in bringing it about. If this isn't enough for you to expand your love and understanding, think of someone you deeply love doing or saying what you have done or said. Tune-in to the appreciation you can feel for this person regardless of his/her actions. You can recognize that s/he had a positive intention behind the act or words. You can give yourself the same understanding and acceptance that you give this other person.

2. **REMEMBER IT'S ONLY PROGRAMMING:** When you are feeling separate from yourself, you can also "instantly double your consciousness" by seeing that it isn't *you* from whom you feel separate—it is your *programming* you

don't like or agree with. **It is only one part of your programming that another part of your programming feels separate from!** Once you distinguish your programming from your essential being, you can expand your love, compassion, and acceptance for yourself.

If you use this technique when you feel separate from yourself and others, you can literally double your consciousness or awareness in a matter of moments. Without the added heavy burden of constantly judging yourself and others, *you can give yourself more clarity and energy for bringing about the changes you want—aided by the power of love.*

TUNING-IN TO INSIDE

Learning to acknowledge your thoughts, feelings, and intentions could be something new. It may be that for most of your life your attention has been directed toward the outside world. Now you are directing more of your attention inward—studying what's happening inside your own mind.

It's similar to the process of learning how to read. When you started reading, you could only make sense out of certain words. That's the way it's going to be as you start looking inward. You will recognize only certain programs. You may be aware of only a few of your emotional feelings, addictive demands, and positive intentions.

As you get more and more proficient at noticing how your mind and your programming operate, you will increasingly recognize your physical sensations, emotions, addictive demands, positive intentions, core beliefs, etc. It's a bit like reading a newspaper: first you see the headlines, then you see the story beneath the headlines. Then you get to the second, third, and inside pages, and then to the want ads, which are in even finer print. That's the process of going inward and exploring your thoughts and feelings. So it can be a long process.

In fact, it's a lifetime process! Your job is to be patient with yourself and to be gentle with yourself. Realize that it is a journey. Enjoy the trip! Don't be addicted to instantly being free of addictions. It's OK to have addictions—each one will lead you onward if you use it for growth!

As you develop skill in formulating your addictive demands and your positive intentions, you will discover that together they give you an incredibly insightful and powerful approach to understanding what's going on in your ego-mind. Addictive demands are like a cancer, and the Science of Happiness offers you the entire 2-4-4 system for upleveling them to preferences. At the same time, your positive intentions give you meaning and purpose for your inner work; they offer insights and new choices for a more loving, peaceful, enjoyable life.

When your here and now is bathed in the knowledge and practice of the two Wisdom Principles of addictive demands and positive intentions, it begins to escalate into a new dimension. Clarity about your addictions helps you shake loose of what's holding you back; clarity on your positive intentions offers you many more avenues to speed you on your way to what you really want—an enjoyable fulfilling experience of day-by-day living.

> **OUR POSITIVE INTENTIONS**
> **TUNE US IN TO**
> **THE BASIC GOODNESS**
> **OF EVERYONE ON EARTH!**

Part 2

FOUR
LIVING LOVE
METHODS

5 UPLEVELING DEMANDS TO PREFERENCES

♥ *So, how do we change an addictive demand to a preference and thus tune-in to our inner wisdom?*

♥ *What choices do we have when we discover an addictive demand?*

♥ *What is the technique of "handling our addictions" that can quickly give us many of the benefits we can eventually get by upleveling our demands to preferences?*

BENEFITING FROM THE SCIENCE OF HAPPINESS

The two Wisdom Principles involving addictive demands and positive intentions are interwoven throughout this book. The four Living Love Methods and the four Dynamic Processes are designed to help us use these Wisdom Principles. Wisdom has a balance between head and heart. A wise response to a situation enables us to look back at what we did and what happened afterward, and then decide we got the most that was "gettable"—given the particular life situation! We could not have done better even if we'd had a second chance.

The four Living Love Methods help you increasingly enjoy the rest of your life as you develop:

1. Your **knowledge** of the cancerous effect of addictive demands and the benefits of cutting through to your beneficial positive intentions.
2. Your **determination** to uplevel addictive demands into preferences.
3. Your **practice** of using your life situations to develop these enriching skills.

One of the beauties of the Living Love Methods is that they can be used anywhere, anytime. You don't have to change your lifestyle or any life situation to use these methods. You do not have to wait for people around you to change so you can create a happy experience. They may never change! Wherever, when-ever you are creating emotional dis-comfort in your life, you can use these methods!

Do we have to uplevel all of our demands to preferences to live a hap-py life? The *Handbook to Higher Consciousness* helps us round out a perspective on this:

```
┌─────────────────────────────────────┐
│  FOUR LIVING LOVE METHODS           │
│  1. The Twelve Pathways             │
│  2. Centers of Consciousness        │
│  3. Linking Separate-self Emotions with │
│     Your Demand                     │
│  4. Consciousness Focusing          │
└─────────────────────────────────────┘
```

Here's some good news. It is not necessary to be one hundred per cent free of emotion-backed addictions in order to experience continuous happiness.... Happi-ness is a general level of good feeling that you generate when life gives you what you are prepared to accept. This general level is not affected *if you can quickly recover* from any experience of fear, anger, resentment, irritation, etc. The state of unhappi-ness develops when an addictive experience goes on and on. This state becomes in-tense when you let one addiction after another pile up on top of you so that you are loading your biocomputer with several addictive models and expectations to which the world is not conforming. *If, within several minutes or even an hour or so, you can get on top of an addiction, it will not usually affect your happiness level.* If you trigger anger, for example, you can actually enjoy being angry for a short while. However, if you continuously make yourself angry, unhappiness inevitably develops because of the continued hyperactivity of your autonomic nervous system, the adverse feedback of the surrounding world, and the overwhelming cumulative effect of subject-object relationships—with resulting lowered energy, lowered insight, and lowered love.[*]

THE CHOICE IS YOURS

In the past we have usually dealt with our unhappiness and our separating emotions in one of two ways: we either **suppressed** our feelings by refusing to acknowledge them or we **expressed** them—in a *me-vs.-you* way—our usual means of handling our emotions when we aren't suppressing them. We've sometimes acted out our separating feelings automatically—robot-like—disdain-ing, scowling, or screaming all the way!

Neither of these two ways of dealing with our emotions has been totally suc-cessful in our lives. Suppressing our emotions keeps us stuck in our unhappi-ness by creating body problems and "grayed out" feelings of depression and low

---

[*] Reprinted from the *Handbook to Higher Consciousness* by Ken Keyes, Jr., page 197, © 1975 by the Living Love Center. Appendix A contains ordering information.

energy. Expressing our feelings can temporarily make us feel better than suppressing them. However, expression often perpetuates the cycle of separateness and keeps us stuck in experiencing the same emotional patterns again and again. And it does not free us from the trap of our demands that create our suffering; it may even strengthen our addictive programming! In addition, it often triggers addictions in the people around us—and this may in turn trigger more of our addictive demands.

Another way of looking at it is that all of our thoughts, emotions, and actions are based on our programmed mental habits. We can change our actions, but that may not change our emotional experience of unhappiness. We can put energy into suppressing our emotions, but we're still left with our conscious and unconscious habits of mind. And if these habits don't change, our thinking will continue to create more separating emotions and more weary battles in our lives. To summarize, when you become aware of a separating emotion (fear, frustration, anger, etc.) you can choose to:

1. IGNORE IT OR SUPPRESS IT:	**EVALUATION:**
Pretend it isn't there. Don't acknowledge it.	This is *not recommended.* It can lead to severe physical and psychological complications. It gives you a phony front. You have little chance to break through illusions of separateness.
2. EXPRESS IT:	
Ventilate it, blame others or yourself, teach them a lesson they won't forget, or take it out on others.	This choice can put mountainous separate-self obstacles in our lives as we valiantly defend *us against them.*
3. UPLEVEL THE DEMAND:	
Change your programming that creates the separating experience.	This choice is the most successful and life-enhancing. It opens the way to the unified-self.

The Science of Happiness shows us how to get at the *cause* of fear, frustration, and anger rather than deal with *effects*. The cause of separating emotions is always our addictive demands. We *move beyond both suppression and expression* by reprogramming the demands that generate separate-self energies—thus eliminating the causes of separateness and unhappiness.

HANDLING YOUR ADDICTIONS

The authors aren't free of all addictive demands—and we don't expect to be. Our lives are a lot more fun, now that we have upleveled many of our addictive demands to preferences. We get better at it as we go along. And it will be the same for you as you give yourself the benefits of these techniques. Although you'll probably never be free of all the addictive demands and core beliefs you don't want, there is a skill that you can rapidly develop which will give you most of the benefits of upleveling addictive demands to preferences. It's called "Handling Your Addictions" and is explained in *How to Enjoy Your Life in Spite of It All*:

HANDLING YOUR ADDICTIONS

If there is an arrow in your heart and you're bleeding to death, it doesn't make much sense to get into a big hassle trying to blame someone for doing it. The important thing is to get the arrow out and heal the wound. Addictive programmings are like wounds or cancers in our minds. Don't worry about where they came from. That's the dead past and it usually won't help you with your addictions.

Concentrate on what's now—the game of using the methods to **handle your addictions** and perhaps gradually change your addictive programming into preferential programming. You may consider that you are **handling your addictions** to the degree that:

1. You are aware of your **specific** addictive demand or demands.
2. Your rational mind is no longer blaming yourself or others for the experience you are creating (even though emotionally you may still feel like blaming).
3. You are using the methods to work on your specific addiction or addictions....

These are three criteria that will enable you to determine whether you are **handling your addictions** using the Living Love methodology. When you are doing these three things, you have taken an addiction from the unconscious phase to the awakening phase.*

---

* Reprinted from *How to Enjoy Your Life in Spite of It All* by Ken Keyes, Jr., pp. 72-73, © 1980, Living Love Publications. Appendix A has ordering information.

As you study this book and the wonderful challenges and opportunities of the Science of Happiness unfold, do be gentle with yourself. If you forget to use these techniques, don't be overcritical or self-disparaging. When you learn to play tennis, you're going to swing at a lot of balls and miss. Setting your sight on your desired outcome, along with continual practice and patience, help you win.

> **THROW OFF THE YOKE OF ADDICTIVE PROGRAMMING. USE THE PRINCIPLES, METHODS, AND PROCESSES!**

6 THE TWELVE PATHWAYS

(First Method)

♥ *"The Twelve Pathways are a modern, practical condensation of thousands of years of accumulated wisdom. They give a minute-to-minute guide for operating your consciousness while you interact with the world around you."* Handbook to Higher Consciousness, *page 12.*

♥ *The Twelve Pathways can serve as guidelines to help us bring our beneficial positive intentions into a present moment experience.*

♥ *They suggest how we can keep our addictive programming from interfering with our insight, appreciation, and love; they give us effective working models to make our lives work better. They open preferential avenues that offer escape from addictive dead ends.*

THE TWELVE PATHWAYS AS A METHOD

The pathways provide an excellent method to use whether or not you have pinpointed your addictive demand. As with all the methods, the pathways work best if used as soon as you are aware that you feel separate. Here are four different techniques for using the pathways. Try all of them and discover what they can do for you:

1. **SAY ALL TWELVE PATHWAYS SLOWLY AND MEDITATIVELY, OR CHOOSE ONE OR MORE THAT APPLY IN THAT SITUATION, AND REPEAT OVER AND OVER.** This functions like switching the channel on your TV to drop an undesired program for a more satisfying one. Saying the pathways will help rechannel your thought patterns from addictive programming to practical, loving programming. They allow insights to come through for a balance of head (rational mind) and heart (compassion and love). Your ego may want to make your inner work more difficult than it actually is. Just do this simple practice. You may be amazed by the results.

2. **ALTERNATE YOUR ADDICTIVE DEMAND WITH ONE OR MORE OR ALL OF THE PATHWAYS.** Use the "Pinpointing Addictive Demands" form in Chapter 3. Notice how the pathways help you to tune-in to your intuitive wisdom.

3. **ALTERNATE YOUR POSITIVE INTENTION WITH ONE OR MORE OF THE PATHWAYS.** Use the "Formulating Positive Intentions" form in Chapter 4. Hearing yourself say the pathways can allow your mind to open itself to unexplored possibilities for achieving what you want most— your positive intention.

4. **SAY YOUR ADDICTIVE DEMAND, THEN A PATHWAY, THEN YOUR POSITIVE INTENTION, AGAIN A PATHWAY, AND REPEAT THIS PATTERN SEVERAL TIMES.** This has been found to be a powerful way to help your mind focus on new perspectives and solutions.

The first way to use the pathways does not require you to know your addictive demand or your positive intention. There is no "right" or "wrong" pathway. Choose the ones that feel most useful to you in each particular situation.

APPLYING THE PATHWAYS

Find out how each of the Twelve Pathways can offer you insights in your life.* The more you imagine experiencing a situation you feel upset about through the perspective of the pathways, the more they can help you glide into a peaceful inner state. Here is an example of how you might use one of the above techniques when your supervisor tells you in front of your co-workers to redo a report and you trigger an addiction that makes you feel angry. Say to yourself:

My positive intention is to feel appreciated.

I take full responsibility here and now for everything I experience, for it is my own programming that creates my actions and also influences the reactions of people around me.

My positive intention is to feel appreciated.

---

* *How to Enjoy Your Life in Spite of It All* by Ken Keyes, Jr. devotes an entire chapter to each of the Twelve Pathways. Reading it can give you an advantage in effectively using the pathways. Appendix A has ordering information.

THE TWELVE PATHWAYS
TO UNCONDITIONAL LOVE AND HAPPINESS

FREEING MYSELF

1 I am freeing myself from security, sensation, and power addictions that make me try to forcefully control situations in my life, and thus destroy my serenity and keep me from loving myself and others.

2 I am discovering how my consciousness-dominating addictions create my illusory version of the changing world of people and situations around me.

3 I welcome the opportunity (even if painful) that my minute-to-minute experience offers me to become aware of the addictions I must reprogram to be liberated from my robot-like emotional patterns.

BEING HERE NOW

4 I always remember that I have everything I need to enjoy my here and now—unless I am letting my consciousness be dominated by demands and expectations based on the dead past or the imagined future.

5 I take full responsibility here and now for everything I experience, for it is my own programming that creates my actions and also influences the reactions of people around me.

6 I accept myself completely here and now and consciously experience everything I feel, think, say, and do (including my emotion-backed addictions) as a necessary part of my growth into higher consciousness.

INTERACTING WITH OTHERS

7 I open myself genuinely to all people by being willing to fully communicate my deepest feelings, since hiding in any degree keeps me stuck in my illusion of separateness from other people.

8 I feel with loving compassion the problems of others without getting caught up emotionally in their predicaments that are offering them messages they need for their growth.

9 I act freely when I am tuned in, centered, and loving, but if possible I avoid acting when I am emotionally upset and depriving myself of the wisdom that flows from love and expanded consciousness.

DISCOVERING MY CONSCIOUS-AWARENESS

10 I am continually calming the restless scanning of my rational mind in order to perceive the finer energies that enable me to unitively merge with everything around me.

11 I am constantly aware of which of the Seven Centers of Consciousness I am using, and I feel my energy, perceptiveness, love, and inner peace growing as I open all of the Centers of Consciousness.

12 I am perceiving everyone, including myself, as an awakening being who is here to claim his or her birthright to the higher consciousness planes of unconditional love and oneness.

I always remember that I have everything I need to enjoy my here and now—unless I am letting my consciousness be dominated by demands and expectations based on the dead past or the imagined future.

My positive intention is to feel appreciated.

I am perceiving everyone, including myself, as an awakening being who is here to claim his or her birthright to the higher consciousness planes of unconditional love and oneness.

Now think of a recent incident in which you felt upset. Choose one of the four ways for using the pathways and take a minute to do it. Afterwards, reflect on any insights that came up for you.

Congratulations! You've used the pathways as a method!

WHY ALL THE STRUCTURE?

As you get into the four Methods and four Processes, you will find specific structured directions for making each one effective in your life. Many of us are quite resistant to structure: "I'm an intelligent person and can do it my own way." You're right—you are intelligent. We know that smart people constitute the audience for this book. And our intelligence creates a problem—it becomes the handmaiden of the ego-mind's addictive desires. Often the more intelligent we are, the more clever we can be at defending and maintaining our separating demands on ourselves, other people and the world!

So how do we get out of this box created by our intelligence? The authors have been working with people for over ten years using these methods and processes. We've tried them in countless forms. We've used minimum structure; we've used maximum structure. And we can only offer you what our experience has clearly indicated: to overcome decades of separate-self programming, we grow fastest when we utilize a specific structure that is designed to head off our usual habits of blaming ourselves or others, experiencing ourselves as "victims," or manipulating the facts of life to fit our programmed beliefs.

We are therefore recommending that you set aside any judgment or resistance to what you may perceive as too much structure in the forms we recommend for retraining your ego-mind. Use the gift of your intelligence to understand that without your patient and diligent use of these forms in everyday life situations, your benefits from this book may be largely intellectual with little impact on your actual daily experience. You may wish to put in the programming that really smart people do those things that get the best results!

MEMORIZE THE PATHWAYS

To maximally benefit from the Twelve Pathways, memorize them word perfectly. When you experience separating emotions, your ego may tend to forget the pathways entirely, or to leave out important words or phrases unless they are solidly memorized. Memorizing them is the best way to have them readily available when you need them. Once you memorize the pathways, you will begin to experience them on deeper levels of insight. *Memorizing them also helps to implant them more effectively in your intuitive mind.* Knowing them by heart reinforces your determination to reduce separateness and increase your insight and love. These pathways can become your friends in times of emotional turmoil and confusion.

If you find yourself creating frustration as you memorize the pathways, and you are telling yourself you "can't memorize them," acknowledge that as part of your addictive programming. Use the methods to uplevel this addiction to a preference.

We suggest that you not paraphrase the pathways or put them in other words. Each of the pathways is loaded with several systematically interlocking concepts that can help

---

TIPS FOR MEMORIZING

Memorize them one at a time (perhaps one per hour or one per day).

Work with someone else.

Put copies around your house so that you see and read the pathways frequently: on the refrigerator, in the bathroom, by the phone, etc.

Memorize them one word or phrase at a time: "I," "I am," "I am freeing," "I am freeing myself," etc.

Use main words as cues, "I am freeing... addictions." "I am discovering...illusory version."

Put them in your pocket or around your wrist.

Draw a picture of each pathway, or imagine a picture of each one.

Imagine gesturing or acting the phrases of each pathway.

Read them aloud before going to sleep, upon waking in the morning, and several times a day.

Put them on tape and listen to them before you go to sleep, when you get up in the morning, or several times a day.*

Put them to music.*

---

* Two cassettes are available that may be helpful: "The Twelve Pathways" sung by Beth (catalog #125) and "The Twelve Pathways" meditatively shared by Bill Lentz (catalog #114). These are repeated several times. Cassettes are available for $6.00 each plus $1.25 postage from the Ken Keyes College Bookroom, 790 Commercial Avenue, Coos Bay, OR 97420.

you create a more harmonious enjoyment of your life. They have been used millions of times and have proven to be a wonderful tool for personal growth. Use them as they are for rapid results.

DARE TO ACCEPT THE CHALLENGE

Countless lives have grown into a new dimension of happiness through the Science of Happiness. Challenge yourself to explore this in your own life. The only thing in your way are certain habits of mind—absolutely nothing else. Your knowledge, your determination, and your practice of the 2-4-4 system all reinforce each other with every forward step you make. The transition from the separate-self to the unified-self can be the most valuable thing in your life. You can give yourself this priceless gift!

> **YOU ARE INCREASING
> YOUR DETERMINATION
> TO BECOME THE MASTER
> OF YOUR EXPERIENCE.**

7 Centers of Consciousness

(Second Method)

♥ *"These Centers act as filters that generate your particular private experience of the here and now in your life."* Handbook to Higher Consciousness, *page 44.*

♥ *The general level of enjoyment in our lives gradually rises as we more frequently choose to generate our present circumstance from the higher, unifying Centers of Consciousness. They may be used as a measuring scale that encourages us to develop the skills that yield a more satisfying here and now experience.*

♥ *The Centers of Consciousness offer us an effective tool that helps us use everything that happens in our lives either for our enjoyment or our growth. They enhance our awareness that we always have choice.*

FILTERS THAT COLOR YOUR EXPERIENCE

Every situation can be perceived from each of the Seven Centers of Consciousness. Your emotional experience of any situation depends on the center of consciousness you use to interpret that situation in your life. When you use programming from the Security, Sensation, or Power Center of Consciousness, your attention and energy are preoccupied with trying to find "enough" security, "enough" sensation, or "enough" power. These addictive filters limit your energy, distort your perception, and trigger separateness in your life.

When you use the programming of the Love, Cornucopia, or Conscious-awareness Centers, you experience

CENTERS OF CONSCIOUSNESS
1. Security
2. Sensation
3. Power
4. Love
5. Cornucopia
6. Conscious-awareness
7. Cosmic Consciousness

your life with love and emotional acceptance of whatever is happening. You are able to preferentially direct your energy toward changes without being addicted to the results. You are able to focus on your positive intentions so that your mind automatically chooses new options that can better help you get what you really want.

Increased awareness is important in making changes, and in this chapter we will be encouraging you to increase your insight about yourself by exploring your emotions and the centers of consciousness that originate them. Some people initially feel apprehensive about contemplating which separate-self emotions they are feeling. They're worried that if they dwell on those undesirable feelings they'll stay stuck in them. However, based on our experience with ourselves and other people, when we acknowledge those feelings and apply the Wisdom Principles, Methods, and Processes, we find ourselves moving away from separateness and toward insight, love, and other unified-self emotions. We also become more effective in making changes we want in our lives.

You identify your center(s) of consciousness primarily by what you feel, and also by the programming that is being triggered. Your center of consciousness is *not determined by what you do or by what is happening.* For instance, suppose you are waiting to cross a busy street with four lanes of traffic. If you feel afraid and are preoccupied with possible injury, you are using your Security Center to generate your experience. If you're feeling calm, enjoying the activity, and are just watching for a break in the traffic, you're using your Love Center to create your experience. Your center of consciousness is always selected by your programming—*the life situation is almost irrelevant!*

THE CENTERS OF CONSCIOUSNESS

Every time you generate your experience with the next higher center of consciousness, you automatically increase your energy, genuine contact with people, and enjoyment in life. Please also note that there is nothing "wrong" with the Security, Sensation, and Power Centers and it's not "bad" to use their filters; the predicament is that they keep you trapped in separate-self programming. For example, if you feel sexual energy and you run it through the the Sensation Center, you have an addictive potential that makes you vulnerable to frustration and disappointment if sex doesn't happen the way you want it to. Sexual energy flowing preferentially through the Love Center does not trigger unpleasant or separating emotions. We aren't against sexual energy; we're just noting that the center you choose will determine whether you'll be on that well-known roller coaster between pleasure and pain!

Below is an outline of the Centers of Consciousness with emotions and typical programming associated with each center. Whenever you feel any of the emotions listed under, for example, the Security Center, that means you are probably using the Security Center through which you filter your experience at that moment. When you feel an emotion which is listed under more than one center of consciousness, such as jealousy or frustration, then you must sense from inside if the driving energy is coming from feeling that you're not getting enough security, sensation, or power. And notice that all of the emotions listed under the Love Center are also experienced in the Cornucopia Center.

We've classified these emotions the way they fit for us. If, for you, an emotion we've listed under one center seems more appropriate under another center, feel free to change it. Also add any other gut-level feelings. All of the Science of Happiness must be validated based on our human experience. What matters here is that you use words as tools that point to particular emotions you feel inside.

The words given in italics relate to this situation: Harry doesn't show up for a date.

1. **SECURITY CENTER:** Addictively demanding what you think will give you physical and emotional security. Some typical security programming and addictive demands relating to the situation of Harry not showing up for a date may sound like:

> *I'm afraid Harry doesn't care for me anymore. I just know that people at school will think I'm no fun to be with. No one will ask me out ever again. Maybe I'm too fat. Maybe he likes Helen better.*

USUAL EMOTIONS WHEN SECURITY PROGRAMMING IS NOT MET:

fear	anxiety	hurt	confusion
apprehension	panic	sadness	embarrassment
worry	terror	helplessness	envy
dread	horror	grief	doubt
nervousness	despair	loneliness	jealousy
despondency	regret	powerlessness	dejection
bitterness	hopelessness	shame	alarm
dismay	insecurity	alienation	isolation
mournfulness	disappointment	guilt	discouragement

2. **SENSATION CENTER:** Addictively demanding sensations. This includes all the sensations a person could addictively desire: food, sex, physical comfort, music, avoiding pain, the "right" temperature, touching, etc. For instance:

I feel disappointed and frustrated because I won't get to be with Harry tonight. Also, I won't have that delicious dinner at the restaurant. Now there's nothing for me to do. I'll watch television.... Oh, nothing good on. Maybe I'll go get some ice cream or make some popcorn.... I'll sit on this neat new chair—yuck! The cat wet it and now it smells bad. I don't feel like cleaning it.

USUAL EMOTIONS WHEN SENSATION PROGRAMMING IS NOT MET:

frustration	discouragement	jealousy	dismay	disgust
boredom	disappointment	grief	alienation	envy

3. **POWER CENTER:** Addictively demanding to control, to manipulate, or to protect and maintain a particular image, role, or territory. For example:

How dare he treat me that way! I'm so angry I could scream! He didn't even call me. I don't want to date him anymore. He's lost his chance now. It makes me just furious that I passed up a date with John to go out with Harry. Who does he think he is, anyway? I'll show him!

USUAL EMOTIONS WHEN POWER PROGRAMMING IS NOT MET:

anger	frustration	alienation	revulsion	wrath
annoyance	aggravation	indignation	hate	powerlessness
irritation	exasperation	hostility	rage	jealousy
impatience	resentment	disdain	fury	malice

We now leave the "lower" or first three centers from which we generate so much separateness and unhappiness, and survey the centers through which we can create an enriched, satisfying experience from one moment to the next. The emotions listed below are nonseparating or unifying.

4. **LOVE CENTER:** Unconditional emotional acceptance of everyone and everything around you. Life is fun! You still have your preferences. You view people, yourself, and situations not in terms of how well they meet your programmed demands; instead, you might say to yourself, "Well, that's what is—here and now." You are emotionally *in the moment* accepting the situation (even though you may be putting energy into changing it). For example:

> *Hummm, Harry's not here and I expected him. I don't want to create any illusions about what's happening with him. Maybe I'll call him and find out. I could go out but I think I'll just relax here at home. I'll have a peaceful evening—and, even though I don't like Harry not coming, I still feel love for him.*

USUAL EMOTIONS WHEN LOVE PROGRAMMING IS BEING USED:

love	satisfaction	compassion	benevolence
acceptance	affection	appreciation	intimacy
contentment	happiness	lightheartedness	serenity
peace	togetherness	relaxation	enjoyment
tranquillity	gladness	cheerfulness	understanding
enthusiasm	humility	buoyancy	courage
calmness	tenderness	closeness	safety
friendliness	harmony	warmheartedness	empathy
delight	merriment	joviality	inspiration

5. **CORNUCOPIA CENTER:** You experience your life as one beautiful or "miraculous" happening after another. You have more than you need to be happy, and you perceive abundance in your life. Everything that happens is perfect for you to enjoy—**or to use as an opportunity to get free of an addiction.** *Your appreciation and gratitude expand as you experience everything in life as a gift.* For example:

> *I genuinely appreciate this opportunity to work on my addiction to being with Harry and to having him be here when he says he's coming.... Now I get to enjoy the time by myself. I can put on a new cassette. I've been wanting some time to myself—now I've got it and I can enjoy being with me! I can write a letter to my friend Sylvia and tell her how much I love her.*

INCLUDE ALL LOVE CENTER EMOTIONS.

joy	richness	exhilaration	fulfillment
abundance	elation	exultation	rapture
awe	wonder	gratitude	bliss

6. **CONSCIOUS-AWARENESS CENTER:** Nonjudgmental awareness of yourself and others in your drama of life. It's a "third" person point of view of your own life, as if you were viewing yourself as an actor or actress in a movie. You do not identify yourself with the roles you play: woman or man, young or old, rich or poor, husband or wife, boss or worker, etc. Playing your part on the stage of the world does not mean you are the roles you play any more than you are the clothes you wear. Both your roles and your clothes *belong to you*—they are not you!

You often watch a movie, with interest, from the Conscious-awareness Center. From this center, you are not emotionally resisting the actors playing out their emotions—even anger or hate. You are just *empathetically* tuning-in to the drama of life with a *nonpersonal perspective*. You may perceive everyone in the drama as ultimately motivated by positive intentions—perhaps as trying to feel appreciated and loved. In like fashion, you can enjoy watching the "soap opera" of your life, including the expression of any programming or separating emotions from any of the other centers of consciousness. When you are using this center, you observe yourself using any other centers with a sense of distance from the experiences. Here's an example of the Conscious-awareness Center:

> *There she is, playing the part of the hurt girlfriend, feeling lonely and sad, thinking Harry has to be here for her to feel loved and enough. She's really into the security role. Oh, now she's into the power role—making him wrong and holding on to that. That's the Harry-not-showing-up drama unfolding perfectly.* Or: *There she is, creating a happy time for herself. When Harry doesn't show up, she's flowing with that and enjoying her evening.*

USUAL EMOTIONS WHEN CONSCIOUS-AWARENESS PROGRAMMING IS BEING USED:

Any emotions can be felt from any of the other centers of consciousness; however, the feelings are observed without judgmentalness—*just noticed but not identified with.*

7. **COSMIC CONSCIOUSNESS CENTER:** Being one with everything: no separating thoughts or perceptions; *understanding, loving, and identifying with it all*—and thus with nothing special!*

CENTERS OF CONSCIOUSNESS AS A METHOD

As a method, the Centers of Consciousness help you gain perspective and distance from your addictive programming. Awareness of these centers helps you realize that you create your experiences by what you are telling yourself. *You know that you can choose your experience.* You can change your experience by using your imagination to move your energy to a different center. When you use the Centers of Consciousness, you gain flexibility in upleveling your addictions to preferences. You don't need to know your addictive demand to use this method. Although at times your demand could be helpful in identifying your center of consciousness, your emotions usually clue you in to which center you are using. The more clearly you label your various emotions, the easier it will be for you to know what center you're in and to gain a conscious awareness of the experience you are choosing to create. General states such as "separate" and "rejected" can be dissected into more descriptive emotions. Go for details. Here are ways to use the Centers of Consciousness as a method:

1. **NOTICE WHICH CENTER(S) YOU ARE USING TO CREATE YOUR EXPERIENCE.** Do this whenever you feel separating emotions. Practice! You will gradually increase your skill in pinpointing the center you are using. Also, stop yourself occasionally during the day and check yourself out to see what center you are using.

    By being aware of your center of consciousness, you will be able to move from center to center more easily. Sometimes that awareness gives you enough perspective to create a totally new experience. More choices; less robot rigidity. As you continue to use this method, you become conscious of the patterns of your security, sensation, and power dramas.

    Remember, you pinpoint your center of consciousness by the emotions you are feeling and/or the thoughts and programming in your head—not by your actions or the type of situation you are in.

---

* You will find it helpful to increase your understanding of the Centers of Consciousness by reading Chapters 9 through 12 in the *Handbook to Higher Consciousness* by Ken Keyes, Jr. Appendix A has ordering information.

2. IMAGINE A SCENE FROM OTHER CENTERS. Use your imagination to notice the many different ways in which you can create your experience of a situation. Choose a situation, then change the center of consciousness you use to experience that scene. You can play the scene in your mind using any other center. Or you can play it through Centers 4, 5, and 6. Or you can play it through all Seven Centers. Any of these approaches helps you develop the skill of being the creative cause and the master of your experience!

CHOOSING YOUR EXPERIENCE

Let's practice expanding our lives by providing ourselves with more choices. First, pick a problem situation in your life. Got one? Now imagine the scene through the **Security Center.** Experience what emotions you would feel, the thoughts you would be thinking, how others involved would seem to you. Imagine how your body sensations would be, and what posture your body might assume. Consider the amount of energy you would have.

Next go to the **Sensation Center** and again experience the scene played through that center. Notice the changes in your body, your emotions, your thoughts, your energy.

Try on the **Power Center** next. The same scene played through the Power Center is totally different. Play out a "Rambo"! Experience all the changes created by this center. Now how would your body feel? You might feel a temporary rush of hot energy. Would you stamp your foot or pound your fist?

Now take three deep breaths, exhale them fully and gently spring

CAUSE AND EFFECT	
Undesired Event Processed Through:	**Will Usually Trigger some Emotions such as:**
Security Center	*Fear, worry, anxiety, hurt, jealousy, etc.*
Sensation Center	*Frustration, boredom, jealousy, disgust, etc.*
Power Center	*Anger, annoyance, resentment, hate jealousy, etc.*
Love Center	*Love, acceptance, happiness, compassion, serenity, etc.*
Cornucopia Center	*Joy, abundance, gratitude, fulfillment, rapture, bliss, etc.*
Conscious-awareness Center	*Emotions of any other center observed with nonjudgmental detachment.*
Cosmic Consciousness Center	*Unity with everything.*

into the **Love Center**. Imagine changing your posture. Smile inside! The scene is the same, but you are creating a more enjoyable way to experience your here and now. Notice the change in your emotions; in your body and energy; in the words that go through your head; in what you want; in how you see yourself, the other people, or the situation. Your perspective is more unified. You choose to regard people with more understanding.

A beautiful way to help yourself get into the Love Center more deeply is to model yourself after the most loving person you've ever known or read about. How would that person respond to the life situation you face? Imagine being that very person. Building a sensory-detailed memory of the unified-self attitude of this loving person will energize your journey toward your ideals. This modeling technique can be very powerful in transiting from the separate-self to the unified-self.

If you have a heavy addiction, you may experience difficulty getting your mind to imagine experiencing "what is" through the Love Center. If this happens, consciously play the situation through the rest of the centers and use the Love Center last. The Love Center may be easier for your mind to use after you have run your soap opera through the Conscious-awareness and Cornucopia Centers.

Play your situation through the **Cornucopia Center**. You might be surprised to find how easily you can flip your mind into a consciousness of abundance. There is always so much to be grateful for! Recognize your opportunity to appreciate the way things are—or your opportunity to grow in new ways. Notice how much energy you feel.

Now in the **Conscious-awareness Center** imagine stepping back from the scene, or rising above it, to observe impartially the drama and emotions that are happening. You have no judgment or rejection of any of it; you are only watching. From this center, you can notice which other centers are being used. You neutrally perceive limitations and changes; you maintain a detached position. Can you pick up on the cosmic humor of your drama?

We'll leave it to you to run your experience through your own conception of the **Cosmic Consciousness Center**. This Seventh Center represents an ultimate dimension in the functioning of the human mind. For some people, the word *oneness* points to this level of performance. Other characteristics are mindfulness, wisdom, energy, rapture, tranquillity, concentration, and equanimity. When these are balanced simultaneously, we approach the optimal function of the human nervous system.

When using the Centers of Consciousness, you may choose to go straight to the Fourth, Fifth, or Sixth Center. In some situations, the change in your emotional experience can be instant. At first you may experience that moving through various centers of consciousness is an intellectual game. This is a helpful start; soon you will begin to make the emotional connections. With conscious practice, you can increase your skill in choosing the filter you want. You can walk away from feeling like a "victim" and greet yourself as a "creative cause."

A ONE-LINER EXERCISE

To show how you can use any center of consciousness to experience the same life situation, let's take a single sentence about an incident and run it through each of the Seven Centers. Suppose your boss just fired you. Using the same remark, "I won't be working here any longer," say your line and act it out as though you were in your Security Center. Did your voice tremble? Now act out frustration as you say, "I won't be working here any longer," using your Sensation Center. Then muster up the rage of your Power Center as you indignantly stamp your foot in protest, "I won't be working here any longer."

Now close your eyes and take three deep breaths to make the transition to the Love Center. Let go of all separating thoughts and turn up your understanding and love for yourself, your boss, and your life. With peace in your heart say, "I won't be working here any longer." Then switch to the Cornucopia Center and let your curiosity, your wonderment, and your adventuresome spirit of life unfold to "illuminate" the situation. Be open to discovering the adventures and benefits that await you as life moves you from one scenario to another. With richness and anticipation in your heart say, "I won't be working here any longer."

To go into the Conscious-awareness Center, perceive yourself and the boss and the scene in the room from the perspective that you and your boss are just playing out your roles in the cosmic drama of life. Watch yourself say, "I won't be working here any longer."

And then from the Cosmic Consciousness Center experience yourself as a part of it all. You are the boss; you are the worker being fired; you are the business; you are the customer; you are the new job that awaits you; you are your family—you are it all! *And from this cosmic perspective say, "I won't be working here any longer."* And it's nothing special!

Right now pick a one-line statement about a situation in your life in which you have felt worried or frustrated or annoyed. As an actor or actress, run the same line through each of the centers as we just did together. Make the most of your one line and really get into the part. Ham it up. Practicing the Centers of Consciousness in this way will help you develop the skill to be the master of your experience and increasingly tune you in to the more satisfying patterns that are always available to you in your life.

PSYCHING OUT OTHER PEOPLE

You may find yourself at times speculating about what center of consciousness another person might be using. If this happens, be aware that you can never really know what center someone else is in. How can you know for sure what s/he is thinking and feeling? You can guess, often accurately. Just keep in mind, that's what you're doing. And when you do guess, take advantage of the opportunity to realize that you can go beyond judging someone based on his/her programming and what center s/he might be in. We all have preferential programming and we all have addictive programming. We can develop our compassion for us humans—even while working to change programs and actions.

Next time you infer that someone is mad at you, try asking if s/he's angry. S/he might just have a tummy ache.

SOMETIMES OUR SEPARATING ACTS
MAKE US SEEM LESS THAN HUMAN.

THE SCIENCE OF HAPPINESS
CAN HELP US SEEM
MORE THAN HUMAN!

LINKING SEPARATE-SELF EMOTIONS WITH YOUR DEMAND

(THIRD METHOD)

♥ *"The key to the Third Method is to consciously connect all of the suffering in your life with the addictive, emotion-backed models and expectations that you keep telling yourself you must have to be happy."* Handbook to Higher Consciousness, page 86.

♥ *To create rapid growth, it is helpful to establish the cause-effect relationship between our specific addictive programming and the separateness, unhappiness, or suffering we are feeling.*

♥ *When this cause-effect relationship between our addictive programming and our suffering is clearly established in our minds, rapid personal growth begins to take place without the mind exerting itself through "shoulds," "shouldn'ts," or the "clenched-teeth" use of willpower.*

DEVELOPING SKILL WITH THIS METHOD

"Linking separate-self emotions with your demand" means you have the intellectual and emotional insight, in a given situation, that *it is your addictive demand which is causing you to feel separating emotions.* With this method, you become aware of the way your addiction—not the outside event—keeps you on a yo-yo between pleasure and pain. This method encourages your gut-level realization that your addictions are the only immediate, practical cause of your unhappiness. We consider addictions as the "immediate" cause, for they are the intervening variable between the life event and your experience (explained in Chapter 2). We say they're the "practical" cause of unhappiness because *you can do something about them!* **You** always have the option to uplevel your demand to a preference. You don't have to depend on others to "make" you happy.

Remember, when you experience separating emotions, it is the result of one or more addictive demands that are not being satisfied. You stop feeling upset when either (1) outside events change to meet your models, or (2) you uplevel your demands to preferences. Either way is fine. Be forewarned, however, that even when your addictive demand is met, other addictions often quickly slip in. So, when you've tried and tried and the outside events don't change enough, switch to the second way to stop the upset feeling. *If holding on tightly isn't working, let go lightly!*

Like most people, you probably have programmed yourself to make your life work only by trying to change yourself, other people, and the situations in your life. Your biocomputer will tend to continue functioning in this preprogrammed pattern even if you tell yourself you want to start understanding that your unhappiness is caused by your demands. To get the benefit of this method on deeper emotional levels, you must learn to consciously overcome your own outmoded mental

> **WHAT WE MEAN BY UNHAPPINESS AND SUFFERING**
>
> *When experienced hour after hour, separating emotions such as fear, frustration, or anger create the state we refer to as "unhappiness." We use the term "suffering" to point to an intense or continuous unhappiness. We look at unhappiness or suffering on a degree basis ranging from minor unsatisfactoriness (such as triggering an addiction when you run out of toothpaste) to extremely gripping experiences (such as great grief caused by the demand that a loved one not die).*

habits. It helps to remind yourself frequently, even on an intellectual basis, that *it is your own addictive programming and not the outside event that creates your internal emotional experience.* This is a neurological fact—and you deprive yourself of power to *be the master of your experience* when you ignore this reality. We recommend against playing God and trying to master the world; just settle for being the master of your own experience!

This method offers you five steps for linking your unhappiness with your addiction. Here are the steps we will cover one by one:

LINKING SEPARATE-SELF EMOTIONS WITH YOUR DEMAND

1. Pinpoint your addictive demand; identify emotional resistance.
2. Explore your ripoffs.
3. Be aware of your payoffs; question their value.

4. Consider how things would be with a preference.
5. Choose, for now, to hold on to your addiction or uplevel it to a preference.

STEP 1: PINPOINT YOUR ADDICTIVE DEMAND

Linking Separate-self Emotions with Your Demand is one of the methods that requires you to formulate your addictive demand. You need to know specifically what you are demanding in a particular situation. Refer to Chapter 3 for suggestions on how to figure out your addictive demand. Then write or state it, with your emotions, using the standard form. Remember that an addictive demand can be on yourself, another person or other people, or a situation.

> **PINPOINTING ADDICTIVE DEMANDS**
>
> *I create the experience of*
> _____
> *(separating emotions)*
>
> *because my programming demands that*
> _____ .
> *(formulate precisely what you want)*

Here is an example that we will carry through all the steps. Let's suppose Diane has this addictive demand on Henry:

I create the experience of frustration and annoyance because my programming demands that Henry put gas in the car when it's near empty.

Now that the demand is formulated, we have a statement that implies that there is a circumstance about which there is some **EMOTIONAL RESISTANCE**. In the example above, Diane could say to herself,

I am emotionally resisting Henry not putting gas in the car when it's near empty.

Formulating what you are "emotionally resisting" allows you to instantly link the unpleasant consequences (fear, frustration, anger, etc.) to the **cause** of the suffering—*your emotional resistance*—also known as your addictive demand. By filling in the statement,

I am emotionally resisting _____ ,

you can "zap" into linking the separating emotion with the addiction at "lightning speed"—especially with some practice! This may help keep your rational mind from chewing over the situation and sidetracking you.

To explain further, when you are running an addiction, there is some situation or behavior (on the part of yourself or others) that you want different. Whatever you addictively want to be different is what you are emotionally resisting. For practical purposes, we call that the "life event," or "what is." "What is" is that which you are emotionally resisting. It may be real or apparent; the point is that you emotionally resist the idea of it occurring.

Pinpointing "what is" helps you have a clear idea of what you must deal with in order to feel peaceful and loving again. Focus on the "what is"—the life event or stimulus—that your addictive programming is making you resist. (Remember that you can emotionally accept something and still try to change it.) Acknowledge to yourself that *the way life is in this moment is not causing you to feel upset or irritated*. There are probably other people who are able to enjoy or accept the same situation because they are not emotionally resisting this circumstance. Develop the insight and feeling that **your resistance to "what is" in your life triggers your separating emotions**. Your addictive demands are simply what your ego and rational mind tell you should be different. In many cases, you are absolutely right! But that doesn't change "what is" in this moment. Do you really think that people who are "right" have no choice but to be unhappy over it???

To better understand the emotional connection between our unhappiness and our addictive programming, we need to recognize the ways in which we are twisting our thinking and battering our bodies. We can notice how our minds "horriblize," "personalize," and "foreverize" whatever they are programmed to addictively demand. We therefore take the next step with this Method:

STEP 2: EXPLORE YOUR RIPOFFS

Become increasingly aware of the full extent of the separateness, unhappiness, and suffering you experience whenever your addiction is triggered. Avoid qualifying or "explaining away" any part of the psychological, emotional, and physical pain you create when you hold on to your addictive demand.

You will intensify your motivation to shift your desire from addictive to preferential as you heighten your awareness of all the

DEFINITIONS

RIPOFF: *A handicap in your life caused by holding on to an addictive demand.*

PAYOFF: *A supposed advantage that is keeping you from upleveling an addictive demand to a preference.*

disadvantages, or "ripoffs." Thoroughly consider all the ripoffs your demand is causing you. Once you look, you usually find that the ripoffs are much more numerous than you realized. If you have recently run an addictive demand, you can survey with interest what ripoffs it has been causing you. How many of these ripoffs on the next page apply to your latest addictive situation?

In exploring her ripoffs, Diane might come up with a list like this:

> *I feel tension in my forehead, tightness in my shoulders and stomach. I feel the separate-self emotions of frustration and annoyance. Right now I don't feel particularly good about myself, and I'm feeling critical and judgmental of Henry—separate from him. I'm using a bunch of energy resisting Henry not having put gas in the car. I haven't noticed that it's nice to have him back home, that now we can take some time to relax together. I'm too busy being preoccupied with the gas situation. I can't think of any other way to approach him about this. It really seems like a nagging issue. I can see a similarity with the way I nag him about other things. Maybe I'm setting this up somehow by the way I react. I'm probably looking at it only one way, and perhaps there are other angles to it. I sure don't see them though.*

You may find that not all the ripoffs listed seem to apply in every situation. It isn't necessary that they do. However, the more disadvantages you can recognize, *the more motivated you will become to uplevel your addiction to a preference.* To deepen your insights even more, survey the pattern of unhappiness your demand has caused in your life. View your *past, present, and possible future unhappiness* caused by this demand. Consider how you have suffered in different situations with different people because your programming has stayed the same. Until you uplevel the addictive demand to a preferential desire, you will meet the undesirable consequences of this demand again and again.

STEP 3: BE AWARE OF YOUR PAYOFFS

We often experience ourselves "hanging on" to our addiction even though we tell ourselves we wish to be free of separating emotions. We cloak our addictions under a smoke screen of rationalizations and blame. We can rapidly punch holes in this smoke screen by becoming aware of the many clever defense mechanisms our separate-selves continually devise to perpetuate the illusions that "the world is doing it to me" and "I *need* this demand met." We call these defense

A LIST OF TWELVE RIPOFFS

AREA AFFECTED:	YOUR RIPOFFS FROM ADDICTIONS:	AS A PREFERENCE YOU COULD EXPERIENCE:
1. Body reactions	Tension, clumsiness, weakness, queasiness, constricted breath, pain, sweat, rapid heartbeat, illness.	Relaxed body.
2. Emotions	Separate-self feelings such as fear, frustration, anger, hate.	Unifying feelings such as love, harmony, peace, happiness.
3. Attitude toward self	Low self-esteem, limited feeling of love, threat, judgmentalness.	High self-esteem, love for self, emotional acceptance of self.
4. Attitude toward other people	Inability to feel close to others, limited or no love, criticalness, judgmentalness.	Love, closeness, emotional acceptance of others.
5. Energy	Low energy, lots of energy wasted in feeling separate about past or future and trying to force things.	Energy released to enjoy life and directed wherever you want it.
6. Perception of what is happening in life	Distorted perceptions, inability to appreciate the beauty that is around you, lots of illusions.	Broader perspective, enjoyment of your here and now, greater awareness of all the beauty in your life.
7. Spontaneity, creativity, openness	Inflexibility, creativity blocked, fearfulness, pushing and manipulating to attempt to make things happen.	Ability to clearly look at "what is" and deal with it wisely—attaining a larger perspective.
8. Humor	No humor: This is a serious, real, and important problem.	You can see humor in the soap opera; it's just part of life—a situation to watch and handle.
9. Cooperative relationships with other people	Triggering of others' addictions, unnecessary ego conflicts.	People's reactions to your preferential love space help create effective problem-solving.
10. Alternatives and choices	Limited perspective, with "tunnel vision" that can only respond automatically and with few options.	Ability to see many choices in life and be open to a wide variety of possibilities.
11. Making changes	Limited ability and less energy to effect change because of a lack of insight and distorted perception.	High energy, clear insight, and love create ability to flow energy into changing what's changeable.
12. Even when you get what you want	Never enough. Demands escalate. Inability to enjoy: protecting and defending it.	Enjoyment of "what is" in your life without fear of losing it. Loving and appreciating your life.

mechanisms "payoffs" because they are the tempting rewards sought by the separate-self—what the separate-self thinks it gains (or what it thinks it avoids los-ing) by holding on to an addiction. Typical payoffs include being "right," getting sympathy or agreement, and getting someone to change. By increasing our awareness of our payoffs, we erode their ability to keep us stuck in our illusion of separateness.

Check out the list of payoffs in the column to the right. They will be useful in helping you pinpoint your own seeming benefits. You may also discover some key payoffs that your separate-self uses that are not on this list.

Initially, there is often a temptation to say, "But I don't have any payoffs for this addictive demand. There's no good reason for holding on to it—it just causes me suffering." While this is true, as long as you've got an addiction, your separate-self is convinced that it must hold on to the addiction for some "valid" reason. Your job is to push through the separate-self resistance to explore these reasons—these payoffs—and to *debate the value of the ego's reasons in light of the ripoffs.* Whenever an addictive demand is at play, there is always at least one payoff.

Below are some of the payoffs that Diane has become aware of in holding on to her addictive demand that Henry put gas in the car when it's near empty:

WHICH ARE YOUR PAYOFFS?

I get to be right and make the other person wrong. I get to feel superior. I'll prove it's unfair or untrue.

I get attention, sympathy, agreement, approval, and/or comfort.

I avoid taking responsibility for what I do, say, or feel. I can avoid looking at "what is" in my life. I don't have to really experience what I am feeling.

People will know that I'm (a good teacher, a responsible parent, a caring person, a skilled bricklayer, etc.).

People won't think I'm (egotistical, a coward, etc.).

I have an excuse for poor performance.

I get to avoid confronting the addictions that would come up if I weren't running this addiction.

It feels safe and familiar to hold on to the old pattern and scary to let it go.

I get to play martyr.

I get to play the victim role.

It feels safe to keep a distance from other people (or a specific person).

I get to enjoy the fantasy. ("Even if I don't get what I want, I still get to fantasize about it—food, sex, looking different, etc.")

I get to share and feel close to other people who have the same addictions.

I feel a sense of intensity. ("I feel really alive when I'm angry.")

I'll get control over myself. I won't do it again. I'll be careful about what I do. ("If I demand to not eat, I won't.")

He/she/they will change. They won't keep doing what they are doing. ("If I get angry enough, they'll agree with me or do what I want.")

They'll make it up to me because they'll see how upset I am and they'll feel sorry or guilty.

I get to be right. I can point out to him that I always put gas in the car when it's near empty. My friend Lucy will agree with me that he should have had the car filled so we could get to work without having to stop for gas. Let's see what else.... This addiction keeps me from having to take responsibility for feeling annoyed and nagging at Henry. By holding on to this addictive programming I can tell myself I have leadership qualities, and Henry will see me as strong and responsible. I'm afraid that if I let the addiction go he'll never learn to think of things like the gas, and I'll have to keep taking care of all that, and then I'll feel trapped. But I can remind myself that I can choose to not feel trapped when I have responsibilities or things don't go my way. It's funny...I think that if I hold on, Henry will finally change—even though he hasn't for the past three years! Gee, I didn't realize that I was holding on to this demand for such unsound reasons!

Important insight: Payoffs are separate-self attempts to convince us to hold on to our experience of fear, frustration, anger, etc. created by the addictive demand. Payoffs feed the illusion that "the world is doing it to us" when our separate-self wants us to believe that the supposed benefits are worth the price of unhappiness that we're paying.

Take note of a catch in examining payoffs: You must look for your reasons for holding on to the *addictiveness* of your desire—not just reasons for holding on to your desire. Your desire's okay—and would serve you better as a preference. For example, there was a woman who addictively demanded to lose weight. She erroneously stated that a payoff for holding on to her demand was that she would be healthier and more attractive if she lost weight. That is a reason to want to lose weight—but not a reason to *addictively demand* to lose weight! On the other hand, one of her payoffs for holding on to her addiction was that she would force herself to change—to lose weight. Once she identified that payoff, she could then go on to challenge it. She soon realized that in the 20 years she had addictively demanded to lose weight and suffered because of the demand, she actually had not changed herself!

Often people use the concept of payoffs to justify why they want what they want, rather than recognizing payoffs as illusory programs of the ego-mind that keep them stuck in separateness. **The purpose of analyzing payoffs is to call the game of the separate-self by picking apart its reasons for having an addictive programming that upsets us.** When we figure out the reasons through the power of our rational ability, we realize that the reasons are weak, irrational,

70

unfulfilled, and/or not worth the price in separateness and unhappiness. Payoffs are like a carrot on a stick in front of a donkey.

One very illusory payoff that comes up often is "I'll get my way." This is what you've been telling yourself all your life. Most of the time you can't change things by holding on to your addictive demands. There will be a few times when you do get your way. *But at what price?* There will still be separation and suffering caused by forcing your way. So you're no happier. You've got what you want and because you got it by force, it sets up the next "problem" or lesson in your life. You still have the addiction. You will have to protect and defend the change you forced. And you won't be happy. The change won't be "enough." You'll want more and better and longer and it doesn't stop... until you stop it!

Step 3, "Be Aware of your Payoffs," will not be complete until you critically **QUESTION THE VALUE OF THE PAYOFF.** In order to spring yourself free from your self-imposed trap, it is important that you ferret out the basic rationale for holding on to an addictive demand—the payoff. There are usually several. Once you recognize a payoff, you can actively question whether you are really getting that reward at all. And if you are, how long will it last? If you find that you're not getting that payoff after all, how long will you hang on to the hope of getting it? You may be addictively demanding to get your payoffs! What are your beneficial positive intentions behind your payoffs? Can you achieve those positive intentions in more harmonious ways? What will you truly lose if you let go of this addiction?

Taking each payoff in turn, ask yourself, "Am I *really getting* this payoff?" Refresh your memory of the ripoffs. In your mind, balance the payoffs against the ripoffs and ask yourself these prime questions:

1. Am I actually *getting my demand met* by holding on to the addiction?
2. Will holding on to the addictive demand bring *inner peace and love* into my life?
3. Are these payoffs *worth* undergoing the ripoffs?

Here are Diane's answers to these questions:

1. *No. Questioning my payoffs shows me that holding on to demanding that Henry put gas in the car has not paid off in the past, and there are no indications that it will change if I hold on.*
2. *No, exploring my ripoffs shows me that I'm not feeling peaceful or loving.*
3. *No, I didn't realize all the ways my demand has been ripping me off.*

As you think about these three questions, you can often decide that the pay-offs don't carry so much weight after all. *Identifying and challenging* the payoffs can be a very insightful step toward freedom from the addiction.

STEP 4: CONSIDER HOW THINGS WOULD BE WITH A PREFERENCE

This step enables you to accomplish two things:

1) Convincing yourself that you no longer have an interest in the addictive demand, and
2) Actually beginning the unified-self transformation into a new preferential mode of experiencing the situation.

Our imaginations are very powerful. When we put energy into imagining ourselves thinking and feeling in ways we consciously choose, we can make those thoughts and feelings come alive.

In Step 4, you have the opportunity to imaginatively try out a preferential re-sponse to the situation. You may find that one sense (such as visualizing or hear-ing) is easier for you to access and use.

How would things be with a preference? If your desire were preferential, what would you see? Hear? Physically feel? Emotionally feel? Taste? Smell? Think? Also, what would be the positive consequences of upleveling the addic-tion to a preference? Positive consequences could include benefits or rewards to you and others.

Let's find out what Diane would come up with in this step:

> *Preferring that Henry put gas in the car when it's near empty, I am more tuned-in to how Henry looks when he comes home, if he looks tired or rushed. I see myself giving him a kiss. I hear what he's saying to me instead of nagging him again. I hear myself saying inside that it's nice to see him after a busy day, that I want to enjoy our dinner together, and that gas in the car isn't as important as feeling close to him. I ask him if there's enough gas for me to get to the meeting tonight—and either way I feel re-laxed physically. If he says there isn't, I lightly yet clearly tell him I would like him to put gas in the car when it's near empty, and I tell him why I'd like that. Emotionally I feel calm and harmonious. I also feel compassion for Henry and whatever challenges he had today. I feel peaceful, content,*

and happy. I smell the dinner on the stove that we'll be sharing together. Some positive consequences of making this addiction a preference are that I'm free of all the ripoffs, I have more creative ideas about how to handle the gas issue, and I'm able to appreciate Henry. I can easily achieve my positive intentions to feel relaxed and loving.

Take note that Diane didn't avoid bringing up the issue of the gas. She decided to ask Henry to put gas in the car when it's near empty, even though she had asked for that in the past. With a preference, she can be involved in that issue while staying open to Henry's viewpoint and feelings. And she can do so within *the more unifying perspective* that harmony with Henry is more important to her than getting gas in the car. She feels physically relaxed and emotionally peaceful.

The all-important distinction between an addiction and a preference is in *your internal emotional experience*, not in your actions, desires, opinions, models, or thoughts. When you act preferentially, you emotionally accept what is happening in your life. You might still put a lot of energy into changing it, but you feel internally peaceful irrespective of the results of your actions. You emotionally realize your happiness is not dependent on getting your desire met.

BENEFITS OF A PREFERENCE
Use your imagination to create sensory-rich descriptions of how things would be with a preference. Involve as many senses as apply. Remember, the more detailed and complete the descriptions are, the more effectively they will stimulate your experiencing these enjoyable sensations.

Sights: _____
Sounds: _____
Physical feelings: _____
Emotional feelings: _____
Tastes: _____
Smells: _____
Thoughts: _____
Examine the positive consequences (advantages, benefits, rewards) of upleveling the addiction to a preference: _____

Since Diane's pattern here matches the five characteristics of a preference, let's review them:

1. She can still want what she wants (for Henry to put gas in the car).
2. She can still try to make changes (to get Henry to put gas in the car).
3. She can still think she's "right" (he ought to do it—it's only fair).
4. She can more skillfully achieve her positive intentions (to feel relaxed and loving).
5. She just doesn't have to feel upset or unhappy!

Once you eliminate your addictive demand, it can no longer create unhappiness and separateness in your life. You are free from separate-self ripoffs. If you choose to put energy into changing the situation, *you may even be able to change it much more effectively because you are using the more insightful, cooperative, and loving unified-self.*

STEP 5: CHOOSE, FOR NOW, TO HOLD ON OR UPLEVEL TO A PREFERENCE

In Steps 2, 3, and 4 you have thoroughly explored the separateness the addiction is causing and the positive consequences you could generate with a preference. You have weighed payoffs against ripoffs. You are ready, for now, to make a choice whether to hold on or let go.

I NOW CHOOSE TO:

HOLD ON TO THE ADDICTION **OR**	UPLEVEL TO A PREFERENCE
CONSEQUENCES:	CONSEQUENCES:
1. Additional supporting addictions may be programmed in.	1. I can still want what I want.
2. "What is" often remains the same.	2. I can still try to make changes.
3. The payoffs still seem real.	3. I can still think I'm right.
4. The addiction interferes with achieving my positive intention.	4. I can more skillfully achieve my positive intention.
5. The unhappiness continues: I feel separate and life seems "heavy."	5. I just don't have to feel upset or unhappy! I can enjoy closeness and love.

If you still want to hold on to the demand, you can continue to use this method by identifying the unhappiness (the ripoffs) that keeps coming up with this demand. In the next hours, days, or weeks, just keep noticing the unhappiness it creates. Remind yourself that it's your addiction that is causing it.

Sometimes people pressure themselves with "shoulds," thinking they will be better people if they become different. Although they might feel happier, they won't be "better." It's helpful to gain the insight that because you are not your programming, changing your programming does nothing to change the **perfection** of you! If you aren't honestly ready yet to uplevel an addiction to a preference, acknowledge that. Often it takes time to constructively alter your programming. Have patience and compassion for yourself. You will move through the addiction more rapidly if you emotionally accept your programming in the stage it's in; you can then more easily take your next step toward gaining the awareness you need. We all have addictions we don't yet want to let go of. When this is the case, love yourself. This is not a race to the finish line!

DOING IT

Now that we have covered all five steps in *Linking Separate-self Emotions with Your Demand,* you may want to memorize them so they are available to you when you need them. Simply use these key words to help you remember the steps:

> 1. Addictive demand; resistance
> 2. Ripoffs
> 3. Payoffs; question them
> 4. Preference
> 5. Choice

Of course, you can always use just one or any combination of these steps in any order. Sometimes exploring the ripoffs alone is enough for you to decide you can drop the addiction or uplevel it to a preference. At times you might want to go straight to imagining how things would be with a preference. These steps are ideas for you to play and experiment with. You can sometimes accomplish *Linking Separate-self Emotions with Your Demand* in a few minutes or even a flash. You may be able to go beyond some addictions almost instantly by just reminding yourself that it's only the programming causing your tension and not the situation. When an addictive demand seems particularly heavy and insistent, you'll probably benefit most by going through all the steps.

With your strongest addictive demands, going through all the steps of this method just once won't be enough. It may take linking separate-self emotions repeatedly over weeks or even months before the ego-mind will agree to let it go. This method is potent; yet sometimes changing our programming, which we may have used for many years, requires persistence and patience. You can always turn to all the other methods too. Do whatever works.

At first, using this method on an addiction may seem like a mere intellectual exercise. Bear in mind that conscious intellectual change in thought patterns is a vital beginning in making the deeper emotional changes you want. As your practice continues, it will reward you with genuine feelings of love and happiness.

The next time you snag on an addictive demand, be open to the "miracle" of insight and love that can happen when you apply this method. You can photocopy and fill out the following pages.

BE GENTLE WITH YOURSELF

LINKING SEPARATE-SELF EMOTIONS WITH YOUR DEMAND

STEP 1: PINPOINT YOUR ADDICTIVE DEMAND; IDENTIFY EMOTIONAL RESISTANCE

I create the experience of _____

_____

because my programming demands that_____

_____

Using the words from your addictive demand, state your emotional resistance to "what is" by finishing this sentence:

I am emotionally resisting _____

_____

Your suffering is caused by your addictive demand—not by "what is." There are probably other people who are able to enjoy or accept the same situation because they are not emotionally resisting this circumstance.

STEP 2: EXPLORE YOUR RIPOFFS

1. Body reaction: _____

_____

2. Emotions: _____

_____

3. Attitude toward self: _____

_____

4. Attitude toward others: _____

_____

5. Energy: _____

_____

6. Perception of situation: _____

_____

7. Spontaneity: _____

_____

8. Humor:_____

_____

9. Cooperative relationships: _____

_____

10. Choices: _____

_____

11. Making changes: _____

_____

12. Even when you get what you want: _____

_____

STEP 3: BE AWARE OF YOUR PAYOFFS; QUESTION THEIR VALUE

What payoffs do you think you're getting by holding on to the addiction? What do you think you're gaining? What are you afraid you'll lose if you let go? Remember that you're examining the payoffs for holding on to your addictive demand, not payoffs for getting what you want.

On the left, check off each of the payoffs that are tempting you to hold on to this addictive demand. At the bottom, add any others that aren't listed. In the right column, make a check mark if you are really getting this payoff in your life at this time.

PAYOFF ACTIVE?		REALLY HAPPENING?
_____	I get to be right and make the other person wrong. I get to feel superior. I'll prove it's unfair or untrue.	_____
_____	I get attention, sympathy, agreement, approval, and/or comfort.	_____
_____	I avoid taking responsibility for what I do, say, or feel. I can avoid looking at "what is" in my life. I don't have to really experience what I am feeling.	_____
_____	People will know that I'm (a good teacher, a responsible parent, a caring person, a skilled bricklayer, etc.).	_____
_____	People won't think I'm (egotistical, a coward, etc.).	_____
_____	I have an excuse for poor performance.	_____
_____	I get to avoid confronting the addictions that would come up if I weren't running this addiction.	_____
_____	It feels safe and familiar to hold on to the old pattern and scary to let it go.	_____

_____   It feels safe to keep a distance from other people (or a   _____
specific person).

_____   I get to play martyr.   _____

_____   I get to play the victim role.   _____

_____   I get to enjoy the fantasy. (*Even if I don't get*   _____
what I want, I still get to fantasize about it—food, sex,
looking different, etc.)

_____   I get to share and feel close to other people who have   _____
the same addictions.

_____   I feel a sense of intensity. (*I feel really alive when*   _____
I'm angry.)

_____   I'll get control over myself. I won't do it again. I'll   _____
be careful about what I do. (*If I demand not to eat, I*
won't.)

_____   He/she/they will change. They won't keep doing   _____
what they are doing. (*If I get angry enough, they'll*
agree with me or do what I want.)

_____   They'll make it up to me because they'll see how   _____
upset I am and they'll feel sorry or guilty.

Your own personal payoff(s):

_____   _____   _____

_____   _____   _____

_____   _____   _____

1. Am I actually getting my demand met by holding on to the addiction?
_____

2. Will holding on to the addictive demand bring inner peace and love into
my life? _____

3. Are these payoffs worth undergoing the ripoffs? _____

STEP 4: CONSIDER HOW THINGS WOULD BE WITH A PREFERENCE

Use your imagination to create sensory-detailed descriptions of how things
would be with a preference. Involve as many senses as apply. Remember, the

79

more detailed and complete the descriptions are, the more effectively they will stimulate your noticing these enjoyable sensations:

Sights: _____

_____

Sounds: _____

_____

Physical feelings: _____

_____

Emotional feelings: _____

_____

Tastes: _____

_____

Smells: _____

_____

Thoughts: _____

_____

Examine the positive consequences (advantages, benefits, rewards) of upleveling the addiction to a preference: _____

_____

_____

Apply the five characteristics of a preference:

1. You can still want what you want.
2. You can still try to make changes.
3. You can still think you're "right."
4. You can more skillfully achieve your positive intention.
5. You just don't have to feel upset or unhappy!

STEP 5: CHOOSE, FOR NOW, TO HOLD ON OR UPLEVEL TO A PREFERENCE

Check the box that is appropriate for you.

FOR NOW, I CHOOSE TO:

☐ Hold on to the addiction   or   ☐ Uplevel to a preference

CONSCIOUSNESS FOCUSING

(Fourth Method)

♥ *Consciousness Focusing is a powerful method for breaking away from old addictive programming and destructive core beliefs (basic unconscious convictions that undermine our experiences of life).*

♥ *This method is enormously effective in establishing new programs in our minds that we now choose to live with. It can help us create preferential programs and new core beliefs that will bring about more love, togetherness, and happiness in our lives.*

♥ *The Method of Consciousness Focusing has two modes: the Affirmative Mode which can be routinely done in the middle of other life activities, and the Intensive Mode which can bring faster results when used skillfully.*

HOW THE METHOD WORKS

If you are playing a cassette and you don't like the music, you usually do not hesitate to take out the cassette and put in another one you enjoy more. With a cassette player, this simple act only takes about 10 seconds. You can think of Consciousness Focusing as a technique that lets you remove a program that is creating separateness in your life, and replace it with an emotionally accepting and loving program that yields more enjoyable experiences of yourself and the world around you.

But changing long established mental habits isn't as easy as changing the cassette in your player. This is because it is desirable for your mind to have a certain amount of stability so that it doesn't whirl around like a weathercock every time the wind blows from a different direction. However, it's equally important that your mental programmings not be rigid, inflexible, and permanent, for this would lock you into the particular programmings you happened to get as you grew up—some of which add to your loving energy and some of which block it. The purpose of Consciousness Focusing is to help you get rid of the relatively inflexible programmings you do not choose to live with any longer, and to replace them with mental habits that create cooperation, higher levels of energy, insight, love, inner peace, and joy.

The Science of Happiness will enlarge your understanding of how you program yourself. First, it is important to realize that you are constantly programming yourself. Everything you tell yourself all day long affects your programming; it is done automatically and unconsciously. A large amount of your programming is put into your biocomputer when you are emotionally upset.

Everything you tell yourself when you are emotionally upset or excited has an intense, powerful effect in strengthening that program. Suppose Dave and Janice are rushing to get to work on time. Dave is fighting a cold and not feeling well. He asks Janice if she paid the electric bill yesterday. When she says that she hasn't, Dave triggers an addiction and testily replies, "You don't ever remember things."

With understanding and compassion, a bystander could easily notice that Dave was feeling bad and therefore replied in a snappy way—just as we all do sometimes. However, his statement, "You don't ever remember things," *may be considered Consciousness Focusing.* Because of the internal stress happening in his body-mind at that moment, this separating statement was being programmed into his mind. Unknowingly he was putting in a negative, separating program that he might not want to live with; it could affect the level of togetherness and unity in their marriage.

When an idea first occurs to you, it's just something running through your mind. It has minimal effect in terms of programming your biocomputer. **However, when you repeat an idea a number of times to yourself, the neural pathway becomes increasingly established. When you repeat an idea in the context of fear, frustration, or anger, it begins to be deeply imprinted in your mind.** It becomes an automatic program that plays its part in shaping the "reality" of the "world" you create and experience.

When you're feeling tops and are telling yourself things like, "I like Mary," or "Rick has a good heart," you are installing programs in your biocomputer that can add good feelings to the "reality" you create in your mind. So Consciousness Focusing works both ways. If you wish to create an optimal life, it is essential that you be aware and *beware* of what you tell yourself—*for you may be living with it for the rest of your life!*

By using the 2-4-4 system, you are now taking charge of what's in your head. You know that your programming determines how you operate both your life and your emotional experiences. You can put unifying preferential programming in place of the separating addictive programming you have often been using.

GUIDELINES FOR DEVELOPING A REPROGRAMMING PHRASE

Consciousness Focusing can help you get rid of undesired addictive demands and self-defeating core beliefs. It literally permits you to put new programs in your ego-mind that you choose for yourself. The new statements you install in your biocomputer are called your reprogramming phrases. *You are most receptive to them when you have first effectively used the Third Method, Linking Separate-self Emotions with Your Demand.*

To use a reprogramming phrase for a specific addictive demand, you have to know what the demand is! Once you have pinpointed your demand, you are ready to formulate your reprogramming phrase. Reprogramming phrases often flow straight from the wording of your addictive demand. When you are developing your phrase, try using the same wording as in your demand. **Make your phrase specific, and tie it directly to your addictive demand.** Then if it feels right, you can add a more general phrase to alternate with your specific one. For example:

> **DEMAND:** *I create the experience of anger because my programming demands that Linda not tell me to empty the garbage.*
>
> **SPECIFIC PHRASE:** *I can accept Linda when she tells me to empty the garbage.*
>
> **GENERAL PHRASE:** *I can accept Linda when she tells me what to do.*

Choose a phrase that will help you move toward the inner experience and attitude that you *intellectually* know you want. *Saying the phrase to yourself can gradually close the gap between how you now react and how you want to feel and think.* So you must clarify for yourself *what you want to see, hear, or feel inside.* The words of your phrase can gradually direct your inner experience to line up with whatever change you have consciously chosen to make.

Assuming that I am ready to consider making changes in my separate-self programming that made me angry, I could ask myself, "What part of my separate-self

83

programming do I most want to change? What words will help me get the image, thought, or feeling I want?" If what I want most is to have an accepting image of myself, my phrase could be:

I accept myself when Linda tells me to empty the garbage.

If what I want most is to hear inside that Linda is okay in that moment, my phrase might be:

Linda is OK when she tells me to empty the garbage.

If what I want is to feel peaceful, it might be:

I feel peaceful when Linda tells me to empty the garbage.

Look inside and discover what you want. Then go for it!

A main criterion for a reprogramming phrase is that it feel good to you. You may feel a change in your body, and might hear inside a response like, "Yes, that's it. That's the phrase I want to use." Don't try to convince yourself of something that you can't or don't want to buy intellectually. *Be sure you can at least accept your phrase on a rational level.* Some emotional resistance is to be expected and will be handled in time as the reprogramming phrase begins to work. If you realize that you are "forcing" yourself to say the phrase as if it's going to make you a "better person," stop and consider a more holistic motivation. The phrase that will work most powerfully is one that resonates within you, that you look forward to saying with eagerness, and that energizes you as you repeat it.

Try to make your phrase concise, pithy, pointed, catchy, rhythmic. Make sure it is not complicated, intellectual, or padded with unnecessary words that don't really add to specificity. Avoid beginning your phrases with "I ought to," "I should," "I should not," "I will," "I will not." These could give your ego a basis for rejecting yourself. "I'll try to" is weak and may not send strong enough messages to your biocomputer. Reject "even if" because it justifies the programming you're wanting to change; for example, "I can feel good even if Randy avoids me." Also, avoid judgmental words in your phrases: "I can love Joe when he's an idiot."

Don't use a phrase like, "I will not feel angry when Mark is late." *Such a phrase works on getting rid of the emotion rather than reprogramming the addiction,* and you will probably only suppress the emotion. Reprogramming works by moving toward the experience you want. *It does not work by training your mind to smother your emotions.* Freud taught us that we create a can of worms when we repress or suppress our emotions; trying to get rid of an emotion with a reprogramming phrase could result in just that.

Look out for any tendency to use Consciousness Focusing to strengthen your addictive programming. For instance:

ADDICTION: *I create the experience of frustration and disdain because my programming demands that I weigh 30 pounds less.*

POSITIVE INTENTION: *To hear inside that I'm lovable, that I'm attractive.*

PHRASES THAT CAN KEEP YOU STUCK IN YOUR DEMAND: *I'll be attractive when I lose weight. Losing weight will make me lovable and attractive.*

MORE APPROPRIATE REPROGRAMMING PHRASES:
I'm lovable and attractive regardless of my weight.
I'm beautiful and lovable just the way I am.
It's OK to think I'm lovable and attractive at this weight.

(And remember that from a preferential place, a person can still work to get off those 30 pounds!)

FRAMING YOUR PHRASE

Perhaps one of the best guidelines is this: Use a reprogramming phrase that gives your biocomputer a concept you want to live with. For example, with the addictive demand, "I create the experience of frustration and disdain because my programming demands that I weigh 30 pounds less," don't use "It's OK to be fat." That's not a program you would want to live with. Instead you may choose, "I accept myself when I'm 30 pounds heavier than I like," or "I'm lovable just as I am." If you can't rationally agree with a beginning such as "I accept" because it seems a little too strong, substitute "I'm learning to accept..." or "It's OK to accept...." Your phrase might then be, "It's OK to accept myself when I'm 30 pounds heavier than I like."

Choose your phrase based on the next step you're really ready to take right now. See if you can imagine experiencing your phrase as if it were part of your programming now. If you can at least flash on it, you're probably ready to use it to develop that experience further. If you seem unable right now to imagine owning that thought, you may need to find a gentler phrase for your next step.

Here are some steps ranging from tentative leanings to clear commitments for the addictive demand, "I create the experience of anger because my programming demands that Kevin not spill his milk."

> *I want to learn to accept Kevin when he spills his milk.*
> *I am learning to love Kevin when he spills his milk.*
> *It's OK for Kevin to spill his milk.*
> *I accept Kevin when he spills his milk.*
> *I love Kevin when he spills his milk.*

The box on this page has a list of suggestions for beginning your reprogramming phrase. Choose the strongest statement that you feel comfortable with right now. The examples at the end of the list ("I want to...") can be helpful if you don't feel ready to use the others. Or create a beginning that seems best for you. You may also find it effective to substitute "you" for "I" in the above reprogramming phrases and talk to yourself, using beginnings such as "You can accept..." and "You can learn to love...." You can also use your name; e.g., "Fred, you can love yourself...." You might benefit from using a name or pet name you had as a child, since much of your programming was absorbed by "that person." In addition, if another language was used by you or around you during childhood, try Consciousness Focusing in that language.

You might now take the addictive demand you worked on in the

BEGINNING A REPROGRAMMING PHRASE

I love...
I accept...
I love and accept...
I see myself as (positive intention) when...
I am (positive intention) when...
I feel (positive intention) when...
I can love...
I can accept...
I can see myself as (positive intention) when...
I can be (positive intention) when...
I can feel (positive intention) when...
I'm safe when...
It's safe to...
It's OK...
I'm OK...
I am learning to love...
I am learning to accept...
I'm learning to see myself as (positive intention) when...
I am learning to feel (positive intention) when...
I can choose to accept...
I can choose to see myself as (positive intention) when...
I can choose to feel (positive intention) when...
I can learn to accept...
I can learn to see myself as (positive intention) when...
I can learn to feel (positive intention) when...
I have the right to...
(Name) is (what you want to think) when...
(Name) is not his/her programming when...
It's just my programming that...
It means nothing about me when...
I want to love...
I want to accept...
I want to see myself as (positive intention) when...
I want to feel (positive intention) when...
I'm willing to...
I want to learn to love...
I want to learn to accept...
I want to learn to see myself as (positive intention) when...
I want to learn to feel (positive intention) when...

preceding chapter, *Linking Separate-self Emotions with Your Demand*, and come up with a reprogramming phrase for it. If you have difficulty selecting a reprogramming phrase, go back to your addictive demand. Check first to make sure your demand is the specific one that is triggering your separating emotions.

Sometimes we have to search for a phrase because we are not working on the demand that is really bothering us. If you feel you have the right demand and a reprogramming phrase doesn't come easily, ask yourself, "Do I really believe that this addiction is the cause of my suffering? **Do I really want to reprogram this addiction or do I just want to get rid of these feelings?**" Don't try to use Consciousness Focusing to get rid of a separating emotion. *Use it to get rid of the addictive demand that causes the separating emotion.* Use it to uplevel the addiction so the addiction can't sting you.

Be honest with yourself. If you don't really have the insight that your suffering is caused by your addictive demand, look through Chapter 8 for guidance. If you don't want to reprogram your demand, that's OK. Don't try to fool yourself. Don't use this method on an addictive demand that you're not yet ready to let go. It works best when you're clear about getting rid of the addiction and you're going for your positive intention.

EMOTIONALLY ACCEPTING AND CHANGING

Here's an example of an addictive demand, the positive intention behind the demand, and some possible reprogramming phrases:

> **ADDICTIVE DEMAND:** *I create the experience of frustration and disdain because my programming demands that I finish the report by Friday.*

> **POSITIVE INTENTION:** *My positive intention behind this demand is to feel acceptable.*

> **REPROGRAMMING PHRASES:**
> *I accept myself when I don't complete my report on time.*
> *I can choose to feel acceptable when my report isn't finished on time.*

Let's consider this inner work of emotionally accepting an undesirable situation. A common objection comes from the misconception that if we emotionally accept something, that means we "make it okay" and therefore don't try to change it. Wrong! **We can both emotionally accept AND try to change ourselves or others.** The actions we take in our lives certainly have consequences to them; it makes a lot of sense to take the actions that may give us situations we want.

So there are two levels on which to play the game of life: One is the consciousness level where we put energy into inner work that enables us to feel happy and peaceful, and the other is the physical level where we put energy into getting what we want, taking positive action, and making wise decisions about the roles we play in the soap opera of life. In terms of the above example about the report, one may have this attitude:

> *While I want to put energy into feeling acceptable when I don't finish my report on time, I also want to do everything I can to get that report done and live up to my commitment.* **I can want to do both.**

The next page has more examples to give you some idea of how you can work with addictions that come up.

THE CATALYST

A reprogramming phrase that we call the "Catalyst" can turn a day of upset into enjoyable hours with peace of mind. It is a *general* reprogramming phrase that has been proven effective by thousands of users over the years in calming a burning mind. When you are aware of "seeing red," of feeling overwhelmed with an experience of separateness, or of sudden trauma that includes the sensations of physical pain, try saying the following phrase slowly as long as needed:

ALL WAYS US LIVING LOVE

Alternately emphasizing each word can add impact and help you remember to keep saying it. You may wish to experiment with using the phrase as a meditative background for your day. It may help you subtly reprogram the separate-self things you may be telling yourself throughout the day: "I wish the phone would (wouldn't) ring.... I'll never get all this work done.... If s/he forgets the clothes at the cleaners, I'll be upset.... Shopping takes too much time.... Why doesn't anyone ever put things back where they belong?.... It'd better not rain.... Food is always a hassle...."

A time may come when a traumatic addiction is triggered and the Catalyst "All Ways Us Living Love" is the only thing your mind can focus on. It then can help you realize the Tenth Pathway: *I am continually calming the restless scanning of*

EXAMPLES OF SPECIFIC REPROGRAMMING PHRASES BASED ON ADDICTIVE DEMANDS AND POSITIVE INTENTIONS

ADDICTIVE DEMAND	POSITIVE INTENTION	REPROGRAMMING PHRASE
I create the experience of anger because my programming demands that I not lose my keys.	To see myself as efficient.	I can see myself as efficient and lose my keys. It's just my programming that says I shouldn't lose my keys.
I create the experience of irritation because my programming demands that the neighbor's dog not bark and howl all night.	To feel peaceful.	I can learn to feel peaceful when the dog barks and howls all night. I want to feel peaceful when the dog barks and howls all night.
I create the experience of jealousy because my programming demands that Margie not go skating with Frank.	To see myself as attractive.	I'm attractive when Margie goes skating with Frank. Margie's skating with Frank doesn't keep me from being attractive.
I create the experience of fear and grief because my programming demands that Dad not die.	To hear inside that I'm secure.	I am learning to accept Dad dying. I matter whether Dad's here or not. I am secure as I let Dad go.
I create the experience of resentment because my programming demands that the groceries cost less.	To feel comfortable.	It's OK to feel comfortable when the groceries cost more than planned. It means nothing about me that the groceries cost what they cost.
I create the experience of impatience because my programming demands that Mark not be late for school.	To see myself as guiding.	I'm a good mother whether Mark's on time or not. I can still guide Mark in wonderful ways when he's late.
I create the experience of exasperation because my programming demands that the computer not foul up my refund check.	To hear inside that I'm acknowledged.	I am acknowledged in many ways when the computer fouls up my refund check. I can accept the computer foul-up, for it can happen to anyone.
I create the experience of sadness, dismay, hurt, and hopelessness because my programming demands that Peter discuss with me how we can make our marriage more alive for us both.	To feel loved.	I want to learn to feel loved when Peter doesn't discuss our marriage with me. I love myself when Peter doesn't discuss our marriage with me. I can love Peter when he doesn't discuss our marriage with me.

my rational mind in order to perceive the finer energies that enable me to unitively merge with everything around me.

CONSCIOUSNESS FOCUSING—AFFIRMATIVE MODE

One of the two basic ways Consciousness Focusing can be used as a Living Love Method is the Affirmative Mode. Here's how you do it:

USE YOUR REPROGRAMMING PHRASE(S) AS YOU GO ABOUT YOUR DAILY ACTIVITIES. Consciousness Focusing can be done entirely in your head anytime, any place. It can be particularly effective just before going to sleep or immediately upon waking in the morning. Breathe deeply and relax. Then quietly and meditatively repeat your phrase over and over, silently or aloud. Some days you may wish to use the phrase constantly. Write your phrase(s) down, put it around your home, in your car, even at work, to remind you to repeat the phrase. Your reprogramming phrase can become the background against which you play the events of your day. Experiment with shifting the emphasis from word to word in the phrase.

REPEAT YOUR REPROGRAMMING PHRASE(S) A THOUSAND TIMES PER DAY. Sometimes a demand or a core belief you've held for years may require the use of a reprogramming phrase a thousand times a day for a week or a month. Freedom is worth it! We found that your ego-mind may make you burn out and lose interest if you say your phrase much over a thousand times per day consistently. If you use it less than a thousand times per day, your ego-mind may become discouraged because results may not be happening as fast as expected. We therefore strongly suggest that when you use the Affirmative Mode of Consciousness Focusing on a very stubborn addiction or on a core belief, you resolve to say a reprogramming phrase of your choice a thousand times per day until you get the results you want. Staying with one phrase per day seems to work especially well. We've experienced remarkable success changing strong programs used for decades when we work with the same phrase(s) or the same addictive area daily for a week to a month. *This happens when awareness of the programming is clear and motivation to change is strong.*

RUN YOUR REPROGRAMMING PHRASE(S) WHEN YOU ARE DOING INTENSE PHYSICAL EXERCISE. This practice uses the adrenaline in your system when you do physical activity such as jogging, jumping, running, swimming, biking—just about anything active and/or aerobic. The activity in your body helps the new program to make a solid connection in your bio-computer. While you are involved in the activity, yell your reprogramming phrase either aloud or silently in your head.

You'll usually know that Consciousness Focusing has worked when you lose your energy and interest in continuing with a particular reprogramming phrase. Or a loss of energy for reprogramming may be signaling that you have not developed the phrase you need to get the results you want. In this case, reread this chapter for new insights. Perhaps you haven't yet hit on the addictive demand or core belief you need to be dealing with. This can take time; you may now be doing the very things that are needed to bring it into your awareness.

Reprogramming phrases are distinctly different from general affirmations. Reprogramming phrases always relate to particular addictive programs—either immediate demands or long-lived core beliefs—that you're literally "attacking" with the new phrase(s) in order to break through separating programming and habits.

We've included a page of reprogramming phrases you may find helpful. Check them out for some good suggestions that may aid you in making changes you want for yourself. If a certain phrase elicits definite positive feelings in you, it may be opposing a programming that you have—and would like to change. And remember that addictions can be about *anything*.

People who use a traffic counter find the Affirmative Mode surprisingly more interesting and motivating. The counter is also a handy way to keep track of the numbers so that you'll know when you get to one thousand for the day. *The benefits of using a traffic counter when practicing Consciousness Focusing in the Affirmative Mode cannot be overstated.* **Be sure to get one!***

CONSCIOUSNESS FOCUSING: INTENSIVE MODE

When a life situation is pressing heavily upon you and you want fast results, you might choose to use the Intensive Mode of Consciousness Focusing. This calls for involving your body and emotions in a way that can cause a dramatic shift in your programming. You must first be convinced that it is your programming that's causing your suffering. Develop your reprogramming phrase using

---

* They are available at most stationery stores, or you can order a reprogramming counter from the Ken Keyes College Bookroom, 790 Commercial Avenue, Coos Bay, OR 97420 for $9 plus $1.25 for postage and packaging.

SAMPLE REPROGRAMMING PHRASES

Notice that they are specific. The ego-mind clings to general positions!

I love myself when Bob says he doesn't want to see me anymore.

I love Phil when he backs out on his business agreement with me.

I accept Kim when she erases my file on the computer.

I accept and value whatever time I have with my children.

I love and accept Jan when she doesn't write to me.

I feel relaxed while I'm caught in this traffic jam.

I can love Ingrid whether she tells me the truth or not.

I can love Dad when he says we need more nuclear weapons.

I can love myself and feel happy when my business doesn't make a profit.

I can accept Barbara when she turns the volume down on the stereo.

I can accept myself when I forget Jim's birthday.

I can accept it when the crystal to my watch cracks.

I can see myself as complete when June cancels our vacation.

I can stay loving when I find that Cindy has been out driving.

I can feel relaxed when John doesn't get an "A" in school.

I can feel high self-esteem whether or not I apply for work at the grocery store.

I can feel happy when Mrs. Delford doesn't give me a raise.

I can feel OK and accepted no matter what Mother's reaction is.

I can feel abundant and secure whether or not my insurance covers most of my doctor bills.

I'm safe when Harry drinks.

I am safe now and it's OK to play the role of boss.

It's OK to feel happy when I overwater the plants.

It's OK for Gary to say he's going out tonight.

It's OK to enjoy myself when the plane is late for takeoff.

I'm OK when Charlie's programming gets angry with me.

I'm learning to love Sarah when she says, "I don't want to hear that right now."

I am learning to accept Heather leaving me; it's just her programming and she has a positive intention.

I am learning that I am worthwhile when I lock my keys in my car.

I'm learning to feel peaceful when Tony chooses not to live with us.

I can choose to accept my single status and the many changes it brings.

I can choose to feel energetic when it's cold and rainy.

I can learn to accept Mom's habit of crying— it's just her programming.

I can learn to see myself as calm about Jama having cancer.

I have the right to feel peaceful and loving when Marty comes in twenty minutes late.

Wendy is lovable when she doesn't record the TV show for me.

Donna is special to me when she doesn't feel sexy.

Nate is not trying to hurt me when he smokes in the car—he has a positive intention.

Ray gives me love and support and I can accept his choosing to go with Scott.

Dad is not his programming when he yells at me.

It's just my programming that says Mike shouldn't say, "That's not what I wanted; do it again."

It's just my programming that makes me act aloof; what I programmed, I can reprogram.

It means nothing about me when Sally turns the radio on.

I want to love Arthur when he asks Jill out.

I want to accept Rob not calling me about Dad's condition.

I'm willing to love Michelle when she doesn't do her chores.

I'm willing to accept the man who just cut in line ahead of me.

I want to learn to love Maria no matter what her programming is.

I want to learn to accept Mother's death.

I want to learn to feel valuable when I let myself feel angry.

the guidelines previously given in this chapter. Then you will need 30 to 60 minutes in a room by yourself.

Get on your knees, either on the floor with a pillow in front of you or on a bed. Lower your head on the pillow and begin to tense your body. This position usually helps activate emotional energy, and it also helps you stay focused on reprogramming.

With the situation vividly in mind, look back over all the separateness and unhappiness that this addictive demand has caused in your life. Get in touch with how fed up you are with all the ways this programming has kept you trapped. *Feel how deeply you want to reprogram these disruptive demands.* Start silently saying the phrase in your head. Begin to build the intensity and breathe deeply. Clench your jaw, tighten your arms and fists. Tense your leg muscles, and with renewed energy, start saying your reprogramming phrase aloud. **Let yourself experience intense, heavy emotions.**

It's fine if you cry and your body begins to shake. This will encourage your body to secrete adrenaline and other hormones *that will help you firmly imprint your new reprogramming phrase.* But don't overdo the crying, for heavy, continuous sobbing can interfere with your reprogramming procedure. *This is not a ventilation or emotional catharsis process.* The purpose is to change an undesired program you have learned. It's important that you keep the phrase going in your mind.

Keep building up the intensity with which you say your phrase. Yell it if you feel like it. Do not scream too harshly or you may strain your vocal chords and become hoarse. You can tense your entire body and maintain a high level of intensity without necessarily using a volume that overstrains your vocal chords. Notice that you are constructively using the energy from your unhappy feelings to help you replace the unwanted program with a program you have consciously chosen to live with from now on.

Keep the phrase and intensity going as long as it feels good to do it. Your energy for a specific phrase will diminish as it becomes imprinted in your mind. You can then switch to another phrase you want to use. Occasionally go back to a previous phrase to test whether you still have energy for it. Go by how you feel.

When you feel finished with this session, keep your eyes closed and review the situation—this time with your new program. Feel the benefits and familiarize yourself with the new inner "reality" you can create. **Appreciate yourself for the freedom you are giving yourself.**

You may want to try using a wastebasket that your face fits into. When you yell into a wastebasket, especially with a sponge in the bottom, the sound is greatly muffled and the neighbors won't be wondering what's going on. It also increases the resonance in your ears so that your reprogramming phrase is more deeply imprinted into your biocomputer.

Reading Chapters 14 and 15 in the *Handbook to Higher Consciousness* may help you increase your understanding of how Consciousness Focusing works. We also recommend Ken's tape "My Triumph Over Jealousy" in which he tells how he discovered Consciousness Focusing while dealing with jealousy in a relationship. He gives helpful pointers on how to tell that it's working, how long to use the phrase, etc.*

Here's a word of caution about the Intensive Mode: Do not use it prematurely. Sometimes people feel eager to get the dramatic results of this mode *before they are thoroughly convinced that it's their programming that's causing their suffering—and not life events.* There are two conditions that greatly help Consciousness Focusing to work effectively:

1. A ripe realization of the ripoffs caused by an addiction or core belief, and
2. An intense determination to root it out.

An awareness of the ripoffs gives you a strong motivation to make a change. (See Chapter 8 for a list of ripoffs.) The more solidly these two conditions are established in your mind, the more powerfully this tool will speed you on your way to freedom from the old rut of separateness.

Consciousness Focusing can help you break out of the boxes that your separate-self keeps you in. It is possible to reprogram years of separating programming in a day, a week, or a month with this method. But remember, most of your addictive programming has been with you a long time. Be patient with yourself. Don't count on upleveling years of addictive programming to preferential programming instantly. It may not happen that way—although at times results can come with astonishing speed. This happens after much internal preparatory work to build an awareness of the ripoffs and a determination for personal growth.

---

* See Appendix A to order the *Handbook to Higher Consciousness* by Ken Keyes, Jr. The audiotape *My Triumph Over Jealousy* can be ordered for $6.00 plus $1.25 for postage and packaging (catalog # 100) from the Ken Keyes College Bookroom, 790 Commercial Avenue, Coos Bay, OR 97420. You may use VISA or MasterCard by phoning (503) 267-4112.

GO FOR IT!

As a brief review, when forming a reprogramming phrase to uplevel an addictive demand, be sure that your phrase:

1. Is specifically and directly related to your addictive demand. If your reprogramming phrase feels "right" but does not relate to your addictive demand, go back and reformulate your addictive demand.
2. Points you toward the image, thought, or feeling you most want.
3. Feels good to you.
4. Makes sense to your rational mind.
5. Is pithy, rhythmic, and catchy.
6. Is free from pressuring words such as "should," "shouldn't," "ought," or "I will."
7. Does not include such judgmental hooks as "I can love Melissa when she's bad."

Once you've chosen a phrase your rational mind can accept, the next step may be to repeat it one thousand times a day to firmly establish it emotionally and experientially in your biocomputer. This enables you to creatively change your mental habit in any way you choose for yourself.

Consciousness Focusing is a powerful tool. You now have the information you need to experiment with it. And like any tool, practice and more practice enables you to develop your skill to get the results you want.

> **BREAK THROUGH TO CREATE THE NEW YOU!**

10 HIDDEN CORE BELIEFS

♥ *Below the level of our awareness, our biocomputers have programmings known as core beliefs that operate in the unconscious mind.*

♥ *Some of these core beliefs are helpful in empowering ourselves with the energies of togetherness and love, and some distort and sabotage our perceptions. The latter disturb our minds, our self-esteem, our bodies, our interactions with other people, and the world around us.*

♥ *The Method of Consciousness Focusing has been found to be highly effective in eliminating self-defeating core beliefs once they are discovered.*

DISCOVERING OUR CORE BELIEFS

Core beliefs are hardened, rock-like thoughts and assumptions based on early choices and decisions that are likely long forgotten. As bedrocks determine the direction and affect the flow of a river, destructive core beliefs are the hidden rocks in the "river of programming." Rocks provide the ground for the river, influence the smoothness of the flow, lie at the deepest level, and are unseen. Our unseen bedrock of core beliefs guides our behavior and determines how we perceive ourselves, other people, and the world.

We have core beliefs that aid us in our self-image, ability to relate to others, and outlook on life. We also have self-defeating core beliefs that often sabotage our resolutions to change something about our lives. We try and try—and yet we can't stick to the diet we planned; or we can't stop undermining our self-confidence by harshly criticizing ourselves in a way we would recognize as unfair if we did this to others. Then we trigger guilt because we haven't lived up to a new

96

program we vowed to follow. The harder we try, the more firmly the core belief persists. We wonder why our willpower won't work—or if we really have any. Oftentimes, it is the unconscious core belief pulling the rug out from under us!

Since core beliefs are unconscious, they are usually difficult to discover—especially if we're not on the lookout for them. We just don't recognize core beliefs for what they are until they surface into our conscious minds. They can often take years to uncover, if ever. When we do discover them, we can frequently make amazing and rapid changes.

Consider the analogy of an iceberg. An unconscious core belief is like the part of the iceberg that's hidden underwater. The related addictive demands we can perceive are the part that is above water. As we become aware of the "surface" addictions, we can use the 2-4-4 techniques to uplevel them to preferences, *gradually shaving off the visible top of the iceberg.* A part that was hidden now floats up and becomes exposed and tangible, and we can work on that portion in turn.

Since our helpful core beliefs permit us to function in healthy and constructive ways, our conscious awareness of them seems less crucial than of our destructive core beliefs. Because these core beliefs set us up for pain and suffering in life, it's important to understand them so we can change them. We all have some self-defeating core beliefs. How did we get them? And how do we deal with them?

Every child acquires many core beliefs of both kinds, helpful and self-defeating. From the first moment of our awareness that we exist, we begin "figuring things out"—making choices and decisions about what's going on, why things happen to us, who we are, how we feel, etc. As we experience life, we get into numerous predicaments: crisis, trauma, injury, feeling abandoned, feeling angry and resentful, etc. It is during those times that we begin to stock our heads with core beliefs that are intended to protect us from being damaged emotionally, physically, mentally. Their purpose is to guard us by making us retreat, attack, or ignore whenever we suspect we might be vulnerable.

In order for the little child to grow up feeling nurtured, lovable, safe, and capable, s/he must be offered just the opposite of any harmful core beliefs s/he takes on. If s/he has developed the core belief "I'm not wanted, therefore I'm unlovable," the child will thrive and grow beyond it to the degree that s/he receives repetitive messages that s/he *is* wanted and lovable. Most often, however, the child with such a core belief interprets unskillful words and actions of the parents as meaning s/he is unwanted. A separate-self pattern repeats itself over and over until the separating core belief is rock solid. Awareness of where the core belief came from usually retreats into the unconscious mind which is doing all it knows to protect the child.

For so many of us, the little child who experienced all the situations in which s/he felt neglected, rejected, put down, laughed at, or power tripped develops programming that remains inside of us and makes us feel "wounded"—fearful, angry, confused, guilty, lonely, despised, or rebellious. And we live out patterns of repeatedly using "wounded child" core beliefs that were intended originally to *protect* us! Until these destructive core beliefs are reprogrammed, they will continue to keep us in turmoil. We will unconsciously set up life situations and events to perpetuate our core beliefs.

Discovering your core beliefs can be a simple process of expressing/writing your autobiography with as much detail as possible to notice the continual pattern of similar responses you bring to life's situations and events. Listen carefully to what you are repeatedly telling yourself about your life. Build up your desire to understand your programming. As the behavior patterns emerge, the key question to unlocking the core beliefs becomes, "What was I telling myself that led me to that behavior or feeling?"

The more we work with our own and other people's core beliefs, the more we realize that most of our self-defeating core beliefs come from programming we developed with our parents or family. No matter how your parents reared you, as an adult you probably have "stuff" at some level about them—even if they have died. This stuff can affect your perceptions and experiences of yourself, your marriage partner, your work, and with many other aspects of your life.

We suggest that you give a top priority to exploring the programming you acquired around your parents. To understand self-defeating core beliefs that took root at this time, you might use a tape recorder as you verbalize everything you can think of about your parents or other key figures in your growing up years. *Talk to them* as if they were there in front of you. Express all your feelings about them. What did you want from them? What do you still want? What seemed impossible? How do you think they felt about you? How do you see yourself when you think of them? Then as you play the tape back, listen for signs and cues of any self-defeating core beliefs you developed about yourself or "the way things are."

At any time, especially just before going to sleep at night, appeal to your inner knowing with such words as, "Unconscious mind, I want to be aware of my core beliefs that set me up for patterns and feelings I don't like and keep me from appreciating and loving myself and others. I ask you to bring these core beliefs into my conscious-awareness." With patience and persistence, you may be amazed by the results you'll get *when you directly ask your unconscious mind to help you.* For example, Penny would set up good things in her life and then limit her enjoyment of them. For two or three years she struggled to understand why this

POSSIBLE DESTRUCTIVE CORE BELIEFS

ABOUT YOURSELF:

I don't deserve love.
I must earn love to deserve it.
I'm not lovable.
To be lovable I must always agree.
I'm not important.
I'm not creative.
I must please others to be worthy.
I don't fit in.
I'm not capable.
I'm not a worthwhile person.
My opinions aren't wanted.
My thoughts are dumb.
I'm a bad person.
Bad things I've done are not forgivable.
I can't do it.
I'm stupid.
I'm not as smart as others so I'm no good.
I'm clumsy.
I'm ugly.
I fail no matter how hard I try.
I don't deserve pleasure.
I have to yell to get anyone to listen.
I'm boring.
I'm not supposed to have fun.
It's bad to grow up.
It's bad to grow old.
I'm not respected.
I can't have what I want.
It's not okay to feel good.
I don't deserve happiness.
I'm not a loving person.
I must hide my true feelings.
I have to suffer in some way to receive love.
I'll never live up to my parent's expectations.
I can't live up to my self-image.

ABOUT THE WORLD:

People don't want to listen to me.
The world isn't a safe place.
The world is an unhappy place.
The world won't survive and neither will I.
Life is unfair.
Life is hard.
Life is full of stress and overload.
Men/women are tough, scary, angry, etc.
People are out to get me.
The world owes me a living.
The government always lies to us.

ABOUT RELATIONSHIPS:

I don't have what it takes to make a relationship
    work.
A relationship will only work with the right
    person.
I'll never do it right.
I'll never find the right person.
If I love I will be hurt.
I'll get hurt if I get too close in a relationship.
All the good people are already in relationships.
I can't attract/keep a good person with my body
    looking like this.
I'm a loser.
I have to take what I can get.
I need my partner.
My partner can't get by without me.
S/he is just after my money.
Men/women want only one thing.
Women/men can't be trusted.
We should enjoy doing the same things.
S/he should support me.
S/he is supposed to take care of me.
It is my job to improve my partner.
I have to protect/defend my partner.
It means something about me if my partner
    is attractive/unattractive.
S/he doesn't understand me.
S/he doesn't accept me for who I am.
What my partner says/does means something
    about me.
Relationships are hard.
Relationships don't last.
People I depend on will let me down.
I take away the energy of the person I'm
    with.
The one I love will abandon me.
It means something about me if my
    relationship doesn't last.
Divorce is a sin/a failure.
I can't win so I might as well "get even."
I'm not meant to have a relationship.
My family must approve of my relationship.
Even if I try to explain, I won't be heard.
I must control my partner.
Marriage is a trap.
If s/he really knew me, s/he wouldn't be
    interested.
I have to have a beautiful/handsome body
    to be desirable.
Romance is only for the young.

was so. Then one night she awoke with an insight about something that happened when she was nine years old. Her mother had collapsed when they were alone together and had died an hour later. Penny had formed a core belief, "I've done something bad; from now on I'm not allowed to be very happy." For the following 17 years, this core belief was unconsciously activated whenever she started to feel really good.

At the time that we form self-defeating core beliefs, they make sense to us as children; later on if we as adults become aware of these core beliefs, we realize that they are most inappropriate. When the adult Penny realized that she unknowingly had blamed herself for her mother's death, she resolved to use Consciousness Focusing to get rid of it. She began using the reprogramming phrases, "It's OK to enjoy my life after Mommy dies" and "I have the right to enjoy my life after Mommy dies," one thousand times a day. Instead of being burdened and limited by this destructive core belief for the rest of her life, in two months she was able to gently yet thoroughly change an unconscious mental habit that had blighted her life for so long. She accomplished this dramatic change on her own using the Living Love Methods.

As adults living with "wounded child" and/or "rebellious child" programming, our task becomes one of effectively recognizing this destructive programming so that it can be unlocked and replaced. Exploring your childhood programming can bring up powerful discoveries about damaging core beliefs. When you get in touch with a hurtful feeling, such as fear, panic, or anger, allow yourself to fully experience your childhood programming. Make the effort to *see* the child-hood images, *listen* again to the sounds and threatening words, and *feel* the feel-ings that generated the "protective" core belief. Spelling out the core belief is an intuitive process that typically happens quite quickly once the experience is consciously acknowledged and supported.

Another way to become aware of your core beliefs is to listen carefully to people who know you well. Sometimes other people are more perceptive about your core beliefs than you are—particularly if they have had similar core beliefs *and have gained their own insights about them.*

Sometimes you can unearth a hidden core belief by contemplating the opposite of a reprogramming phrase that strongly appeals to you. For example, if you like the reprogramming phrase "I can forgive myself," check out the opposite: "I can't forgive myself." Does it fit?   If so, you've discovered a destructive core belief that is limiting your happiness.

The preceding page has a list of some sample core beliefs. You may be able to discover some of your unwanted core beliefs by experiencing your personal reaction to these possibilities as you slowly read through them and "try them on."

100

The idea is to keep exploring, keep shaving the iceberg. If you're determined to discover your unconscious programming, you will.

CHANGING CORE BELIEFS

Once you've discovered a core belief that has been deeply influencing your inner experiences, the next step is to begin reprogramming it. There are several ways in which deep-seated, previously unconscious programming can be changed. Therapists skilled in Neuro-Linguistic Programming techniques can help. The Harmonizing Process used at the Ken Keyes College can be effective in reducing or eliminating inner conflict caused by self-defeating core beliefs. Hypnosis can be effective at the unconscious level.

One way to change a destructive core belief is to know which influences in your life are reinforcing it. You can start to recognize that TV or movies can have a hypnotic influence and may be subtly creating programming you don't want (or that you do want). Perhaps more importantly, your unconscious mind can be deeply influenced by the programming of groups and individuals with whom you identify and interact. You can be powerfully programmed by contact with people doing generous and noble things.

When you become aware of core beliefs you wish to change, you increasingly detect influences that have previously sustained those beliefs. You can even begin to use such influences as reminders to work on your core beliefs. As an example, suppose you've been socializing with people who have programming that high-fashion clothing is a symbol of self-worth. You buy into this programming and find yourself feeling like you're "somebody" only when you dress expensively and "stylishly." Then you recognize this core belief and decide you want to change it to make your self-esteem independent of your clothes game. You successfully use phrases such as, "I'm OK whatever I wear." Now you can still be with the "stylish" set, and the hypnotic effect of designer fashions will no longer support your previous core belief. You can even dress yourself up, and it's just a game—the clothes game. It's not "who you are" anymore when you get rid of the core belief. So you don't necessarily have to change your friends to grow—you just change your core beliefs! And don't let your ego-mind trap you in separate-self righteousness or judgmentalness now that you're "above it all." Do any inner work needed to keep your love unconditional.

HOW WE GENERATE OUR EXPERIENCE

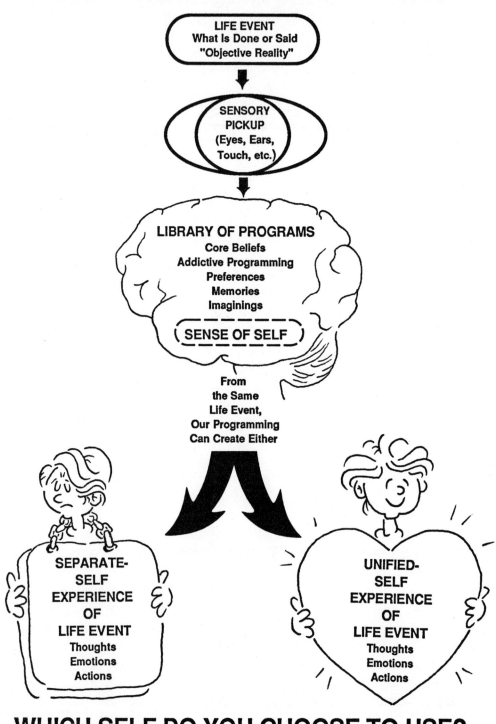

WHICH SELF DO YOU CHOOSE TO USE?

PREVENTIVE AWARENESS

Whatever you tell yourself when you are emotionally upset or excited makes changes in your mind! This happens whether you realize it or not. The more emotionally caught up you are, the more firmly you program in what you're thinking or saying. For instance, **it can sometimes take days of Affirmative Consciousness Focusing to get rid of the separate-self programming you unknowingly install by a few minutes of what you tell yourself when you are extremely upset!**

It is so unfortunate that most people destroy their happiness by not being aware of how their minds work, and what is driving them. For example, suppose several times you think to yourself *when you're deeply upset,* "Norman is mean to me." This can become a part of the programming through which you perceive Norman in the future. It can begin an internal change in your mind that results in ruining the accuracy of your observations. It can make you "hear" things differently from what Norman actually says; you may begin to perceive meanness in Norman when none is intended. You may begin to isolate yourself from a person who could add a lot of enjoyment to your life; you may box yourself into separate-self illusions that fetter your ability to grow. You won't know this distortion is happening any more than a blind man can see his own hand. *You aren't doing this intentionally.*

Your lack of understanding about how Consciousness Focusing works in the Intensive Mode can unwittingly poison your mind. Remember: You are using the Intensive Mode of Consciousness Focusing whenever you make yourself angry and are thinking and feeling separate-self thoughts! You have been using Consciousness Focusing all of your life. Now you can consciously use this powerful technique to put in unified-self programming and gradually eliminate your separate-self stuff.

GETTING RESULTS

One of the most dependable do-it-yourself methods we know to reprogram your unconscious mind is the Consciousness Focusing technique explained in Chapter 9. We suggest that you use the Affirmative Mode of Consciousness Focusing and repeat your reprogramming phrase one thousand times a day. Use the counter for more effectiveness.

It could also be valuable to put your reprogramming phrases on an endless loop cassette or use an auto-reverse tape player. Every night as you sleep you can

CAN YOU USE ANY OF THESE PHRASES?

The following is a list of phrases that different people have developed, used, and benefited from. While some of these phrases originated from specific demands, they all combat self-defeating core beliefs. Perhaps some of them will spark ideas for phrases you can use on specific demands and/or core beliefs.

I am beautiful, capable, and lovable.
I am a lovable and worthy person.
I appreciate and love myself!
My life is unfolding perfectly.
The love I give to others I also can offer to myself.
I can live a nurturing, exciting, and creative life.
I am creating the experience of love in my life.
My love comes from me.
My father and I have the same positive intentions.
I am capable and willing to handle my fears as they come up one at a time.
Love is more important than work.
I love my brothers and sisters unconditionally.
I can shine my light gently every moment of every day.
I bring others out.
I love myself when I want to feel loved.
I can forgive myself.
I can forgive (name) who acts as my mirror.
I can love my mom and know she is an awakening being.
I can learn how to care for my body in a loving and gentle manner.
I am learning to flow joyfully in the present moment.
I can accept imperfection.
My love flows freely to one and all.
I always do my best.
The universe loves me.
I am acceptable and I am open to new forms of being acknowledged.
I can accept the past and welcome the future.
I am appreciating (name) more and more every day.
I'm OK just the way I am.
I deserve to feel good.
I am learning to see the beauty of my life.
I am all I need to be.
I am creative, loving, and nurturing.
I find my life satisfying and rewarding.

I can learn to accept and love everyone unconditionally—including myself.
I can ask for what I want with love in my heart.
I am the source of my security and self-esteem.
I always have abundance.
I am a powerful, creative being who now chooses to love, nurture, and heal him/herself.
Where I am now is perfect for my growth.
I can let others love me the way I am.
There is nothing I have to do to feel loved.
I am open to new forms of loving relationships.
I am open to new forms of being acknowledged.
I deserve to be healthy.
I am a worthwhile person and there is a place for me.
I am lovable because I'm here.
I can feel good doing the things I'm skilled at.
I am learning to support myself with love.
I can make my life work by choosing love instead of fear.
I can learn to feel loved when I remember Daddy's positive intention.
It's just my old programming that played the victim in relationships.
My love is flowing gracefully.
I release the past and now choose a life of love and fulfillment.
I don't have to be sick to get nurtured.
I am worthy of a loving relationship.
My world is safe and friendly.
I can be gentle with myself.
I can feel supported even when I don't meet my models of perfection.
My guilt doesn't help anyone.
I stand tall whether or not I receive my mom's approval.
I am learning to get in touch with my feelings.
I can accept praise and attention at any time.
I'm beautiful when (name) spends time with others.
I have the right to live as I want.
What somebody else does and says means nothing about me.

104

run the tape using a pillow speaker. Thus during slumber, you can slowly alter self-defeating core beliefs. The phrases you've chosen can sink into your unconscious mind as you input them night after night.

As you know, the key to effective reprogramming lies in precisely developing your phrases. It may take many trials to hit on the insight that creates the exact phrase you need to make the change you want. For several months Aura, one of our trainers, used the Affirmative Mode of Consciousness Focusing to work on an unwanted core belief. She stated her core belief this way: "My father doesn't want me and I'm not worthy of being accepted." Here are the phrases that she tried and successfully used to get rid of the destructive core belief that was affecting her self-confidence:

> *I am acceptable to me.*
> *My father's love was so much more than his programming.*
> *I can love myself with or without my father's approval.*
> *I don't need my father's approval to love myself.*
> *I can know my father wanted me when his programming was unskillful.*

The preceding page may give you some ideas for reprogramming phrases. Change any words that don't feel totally flowing to you. Keep molding your phrase until it is approved by your rational mind *and also emotionally feels like the words you want to own.*

When you are attempting to create a workable reprogramming phrase, acknowledge your programming that takes the shape of an "inner child" and "consult" it with respect and appreciation. If in any way the "inner child" feels threatened or abandoned by the phrase, you will experience something less than a resonating, energizing "YES!" experience when you say the phrase. If you're forcing yourself to say it, you're likely ignoring, resisting, or "persecuting" the inner child programming with words that deepen the internal conflict, and the inner response will be one of resistance.

Examine carefully any change your mind spontaneously slips in as you use a phrase with your counter. It may be an important and helpful change suggested by your unconscious mind—or it may be a diversion of your separate-self, trying to keep the old program intact. Creatively stay on the alert for words that *feel best to your unified-self.* It's your neurons you're working with. Your core beliefs must be unlocked by key words that correlate with ones you installed and used as a child years ago. No doubt the "inner child" will feel supported, nurtured, and *relieved* to give up the core belief. As its various wounds are healed, you can experience feeling whole, fully capable, and joyfully enthusiastic about being with life in the here and now.

Most of the time when a person has discovered a core belief, and s/he really wants to get rid of it, even deep-seated programs that have been operating for decades can be reprogrammed in a few days or weeks using the Affirmative Mode with a reprogramming counter. If results are not achieved within two months, s/he should then look for a core belief *that locks in the core belief being worked on.* Let's say you have a core belief that "people will cheat me." This normally might be reprogrammed by a phrase such as, "Most people are honest and trustworthy." Suppose that doesn't work. You may have a locking core belief such as, "I must never stop thinking that people will cheat me." If a core belief lock is suspected, you might try a reprogramming phrase like, "It's safe to consider that most people are trustworthy." Play detective and creatively investigate—and remove—any culprit core beliefs.

Most people are locked in for their entire lives with whatever set of core beliefs they program in during their ups and downs of childhood. But you do not have to endure a life that has been damaged by deep-seated programming. Consciousness Focusing gives you a wonderful opportunity to effectively modify destructive core beliefs that you've become aware of. You can own the ideas that you consciously choose today to shape your adult life. You can choose the vistas that you want to see. You can choose the internal thoughts that you want to hear. You can feel the way you want to feel. Remember the little engine that could? It kept saying to itself, "I *think* I can, I *think* I can." And it could! You can too.

Congratulations on your voyage of self-discovery! Watch your life change as you root out destructive core beliefs.

YOU CREATE YOUR WORLD.

11 ADDICTIVE SNARLS

♥ *When we have a number of addictive demands that we are not handling, our minds begin to approach overload.*

♥ *As an alternative to breaking down from an addictive overload, our minds have a mechanism that grays out our awareness of addictive demands and the emotional responses that they trigger.*

♥ *By being aware of these overload mechanisms of our minds, we can notice them and deal with them more skillfully.*

WHAT ADDICTIVE SNARLS DO TO US

When we don't pay attention to our feelings, addictions begin to pile up. When we don't handle our addictions one by one, they may build to a point of emotional overload. When this happens we "blow a fuse" and shut down emotionally. We remain "grayed out" or feel an ongoing level of anxiety until we reduce the addictive overload.

It's our observation that in general the human body-mind can do a good job dealing with *one addictive demand at a time*. The introduction of a second or third addictive demand rapidly develops overload. For example, you might be coping well with demands regarding an overdraft on a checking account. Now suppose in addition you trigger strong demands that your father not lecture you on what you're doing with your life. Your stress level may increase so that $1 + 1 = 3$ instead of $1 + 1 = 2$, and you suddenly feel bogged down.

We call it an "addictive snarl" when our biocomputers snag on strong multiple or conflicting addictions. Addictive snarls are created when what's really bothering us seems too overwhelming. They're often perpetuated by the conflict set up by hidden core beliefs. Our emotional state at these times may be referred to as depression, free-floating anxiety, generalized boredom, feeling inadequate, or low energy. We're aware of feeling separate from ourselves and others. We know we're definitely not enjoying life. Yet we are not aware of any specific addiction that may be causing this moodiness. When we think back over the situations and people we've been interacting with, we may not be able to zero in on any incidents significant enough to have triggered this mental state.

When faced with an addictive snarl, let's always be aware that the mind affects the body and, reciprocally, the body affects the mind; they interact as a whole. We can work more effectively on depression, mood swings, and low energy when all four parts of the Science of Happiness are used: (1) **supporting your body** (through exercise, nutrition, and understanding your biochemical sensitivities), (2) **guiding your mind** with the Tools for Thinking, (3) **the Living Love 2-4-4 techniques**, and (4) giving your life the many benefits of **helping others.***

WHAT YOU CAN DO WITH A SNARL

Here are some suggestions for untangling an addictive snarl and getting back to the business of enjoying your life:

1. Say the pathways slowly and meditatively, one by one, aloud if you can. If you still feel uncomfortable when you finish, keep on repeating the pathways until you feel calmer inside.

2. Take several deep, deep breaths and let yourself relax. Let your mind travel back to focus on the time when the confusion or depression began. What was happening when you began to feel upset or uncomfortable? Then after consideration, pinpoint one specific addictive demand. Identify your positive intention and use one or more of the methods.

3. To find out what's bothering you, make a list of all of your demands—heavy ones, small "niggles," subtle addictions. List all the things that you would like changed in your life. When you have finished your list, choose the one specific addictive demand that has the most emotional energy—the

---

* For more information on the Science of Happiness, see pages vi and vii in the introduction of this book.

108

one which upsets you the most. Work on that demand using one or more of the methods.

4. Do an EIP (explained in Chapter 14) using the situation which you are now upset about. The EIP is an excellent process for sorting through your addictive programming to select addictive demands. You may wish to explore your programming deeply by writing out ten pages of Step C, "What Am I Telling Myself?"

Practice! Practice! Practice! The above suggestions can help you handle an addictive overload. You may also find it helpful to review the section "Handling Your Addictions" in Chapter 5. By skillfully using the 2-4-4 techniques of the Science of Happiness, you can unravel addictive snarls that are causing depression, anxiety, or "grayed out" feelings.

(**ENJOY YOUR JOURNEY!**)

Part 3

FOUR DYNAMIC PROCESSES

12 FROM SEPARATENESS TO HARMONY

♥ *We've described the two Wisdom Principles and the four Living Love Methods. We'll now round out this part of the Science of Happiness with four Dynamic Processes that can help us deal with difficult life situations.*

♥ *Each of these processes is designed to do a specific job for us. We can use them in our daily lives—often right on the spot.*

♥ *The four Processes are based on the Principles and Methods. The effectiveness of the processes in our lives increases as we develop skill in understanding and using the techniques described in Parts 1 and 2 of this book.*

FOUR DYNAMIC PROCESSES

Here is a brief outline of the third part of the 2-4-4 system:

1. **CHOICE PROCESS:** A simple and effective process to help you open up to choices and alternatives in your life. As you find creative new ways to achieve your positive intention, you take a giant step toward the insight, love, inner peace, and happiness you are seeking.

2. **EXPLORATION-INSIGHT PROCESS (EIP):** A step-by-step process to help you sort through your addictive programming, perceive "reality" more clearly, discover exactly what you are telling yourself that causes your separateness, check whether your reaction is appropriate to the triggering incident, pinpoint specific addictive demands, tune-in to your positive intention, and then use one or more of the methods to uplevel the demands to preferences.

3. **SHARING OF SPACE (SOS):** This process may be used when you feel separate from another person. You first use the methods to uplevel your addictive demand(s). You then share using the SOS form in order to (1) take responsibility for having created the separateness you feel, and (2) break through the illusion of separateness (à la Seventh Pathway) that *your programming* has been creating toward this person. Thus in a spirit of togetherness, you both listen to the programming that has been blocking you from emotional acceptance.

4. **CONSCIOUS CONFRONTATION PROCESS:** A most satisfying way of living your life is to have a free choice to "hold on tightly" or "let go lightly." "Holding on tightly" means asking for what you want and trying to get it. The Conscious Confrontation Process offers you an excellent way to "hold on tightly"—*to try to get others to change so that they fit your models.*

    Please note that the four methods and the other three processes are particularly designed to help you enjoy your life—regardless of whether people or situations change as you wish. They encourage you to develop your ability to "let go lightly," to remain internally peaceful whether or not you get what you want.

Having progressed this far in *Gathering Power Through Insight and Love*, you are well on your way in one of most challenging adventures of your life. By increasing your skill in integrating the two Wisdom Principles, the four Living Love Methods, and the four Dynamic Processes of the Science of Happiness, your life will grow into a new dimension of love, enjoyment, and service to the world.

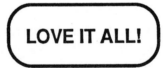

LOVE IT ALL!

13 CHOICE PROCESS

♥ *We've got a problem. We've tried "everything" and it won't go away. The Choice Process can be used to help us break through.*

♥ *The Choice Process assists us when we're stuck in the rut of trying to change something that doesn't seem to be changeable in our lives right now. It helps us explore how to get what we really want instead of beating our heads against a brick wall when our lives are not ready, willing, or able to give us what we have been trying so hard to get.*

♥ *The Choice Process gives us new options to bypass a specific addictive goal. These new approaches can help us achieve the beneficial intentions that locked our attention on the addictive goals to begin with.*

HOW IT WORKS

The box on the right lists the three steps of the Choice Process. You will notice that the first two steps help you focus the power of the two Wisdom Principles on the life situation you are dealing with. You will be using the techniques explained in Chapter 3 for "Pinpointing Addictive Demands" and in Chapter 4 for "Formulating Positive Intentions." The Choice Process can help you empower yourself to go from "victim" to "creative cause" of your experience of your life.

> **CHOICE PROCESS**
>
> A. *Pinpoint your addiction: I create the experience of __(separating emotions)__ because my programming demands that __(what you want)__.*
> B. *My positive intention behind this addiction is to see myself as, OR to hear inside that I'm, OR to feel __(internal experience)__.*
> C. *Three new ways to achieve this positive intention are:*
>   1. _____
>   2. _____
>   3. _____

Step C of the Choice Process invites you to use your inner wisdom and creativity to come up with three new ways to achieve your positive intention. The only guideline for choosing your three new ways is this:

CHOOSE WAYS YOU CAN INITIATE AND MAINTAIN BY YOURSELF.

This criterion keeps you from destroying your inner power by setting up another round of blaming or feeling hopeless; this can happen if you choose new ways that require other people or the world to change for you to actualize your positive intention. Here is an example that *does not meet* the initiate-and-maintain guideline: "Get Kathy to take me to dinner tonight." But notice how this one *does*: "Ask Kathy to take me to dinner tonight." The asking is something that you can initiate and maintain by yourself—getting her to do it depends on her! Once you start using this empowering guideline, you will find it easy to sort out which creative new ways can be initiated and maintained by yourself— thus avoiding choices that can set you up for feeling "victimized" by others.

Your mind already contains the three new ways you need. You are the world's foremost authority on your own experience and the information stored in the depths of your unconscious mind. You *intuitively* know the best ways to handle every situation in your life. Because of the programmed addictive demands you've acquired, you cannot always easily access these in your conscious mind and use them. The Choice Process helps you realize your potential by using the two Wisdom Principles to assist you in accessing your inner wisdom.

Be creative! The new ways can involve action, inner work, or both. Anytime you are feeling separating emotions because an addictive demand is not being met, you can rechannel your energy into new, more satisfying ways to achieve your positive intention behind the demand. It can be so simple.

Developing your skill with this dynamic process can help you discover effective choices and alternatives in your life. You can use the Choice Process to take a giant step that moves you away from continuing a cycle of separateness and toward creating the experience you want. Notice that your addiction has not helped you achieve your positive intention. Most likely continuing to run the addiction just perpetuates your separateness. With this process, you direct your mind to discover more skillful ways to create the internal experience you're really after. You may wish to put the three steps of the Choice Process in your memory so they will be there when you want to apply them.

EXAMPLES OF THE CHOICE PROCESS

Here's how the three steps of the Choice Process can be used:

A. I create the experience of ___*(anger and resentment)*___ because my programming demands that ___*(Don not spend money on carpeting)*___.

B. My positive intention behind this addiction is ___*(to hear inside that I'm secure)*___.

C. Three new ways to achieve this positive intention are:

1. *To remind myself that Don's buying the carpet does not create my insecurity—only my programming does.* (Linking Separate-self Emotions with your Demand)

2. *To consider what I do have and tell myself that we have enough money for what we need and that my fear and worry come from running tapes about my world from the Security Center.* (Centers of Consciousness)

3. *To turn to less expensive forms of entertainment until the carpeting is paid off.*

Here's another example of how to use the Choice Process:

A. I create the experience of ___*(fear, panic, and disappointment)*___ because my programming demands that ___*(Al have called the Chicago office)*___.

B. My positive intention behind this addiction is ___*(to feel relaxed)*___.

C. Three new ways to achieve this positive intention are:

1. *Say the Fourth Pathway to myself and experience this situation with the programming of that pathway: I always remember that I have everything I need to enjoy my here and now—unless I am letting my consciousness be dominated by demands and expectations based on the dead past or the imagined future.*

2. *Take a few deep breaths, shake out tension, and then relax totally for 3 minutes.*

3. *Ask Al to give me a shoulder massage while he explains why he didn't make the call.*

Achieving your positive intention is often more valuable than getting your demand satisfied! Let's suppose in this situation that Al did make the call—only to get unwanted bad news. It might be difficult to feel relaxed—even though the original demand was satisfied! Achieving your positive intention empowers you by putting **YOU** back in charge of your emotions. And sometimes the Choice Process will enable you to access a creative, loving new way to change a life event. You might even get your addiction satisfied! But don't hold your breath until it happens!

Now turn back to the Choice Process form at the beginning of this chapter and use it with one of your demands.

POINTS TO REMEMBER

The value of the Choice Process is that it helps you choose new approaches for achieving your positive intentions. You are free from depending only upon your demands being satisfied in order to feel peaceful, happy, or secure! Here are some more ideas to keep in mind:

CREATIVITY: Let yourself be as creative as you can in thinking of new alternatives!

NEW PERSPECTIVES: Make sure the three new ways relate to achieving your positive intention. *Do not list only ways to get what you are addictively demanding.* The three new ways can involve an outward action or can take place only in your mind. They can include ways to change your perspective, ways for changing "what is," or specific Living Love Methods you want to use. Including a pathway or other method in Step C may directly and skillfully help you to achieve the desired change in your internal experience. Using a method as a new way may also help you realize that you already have your positive intention met and that your addiction is just blocking you from realizing it.

INTERNAL EXPERIENCE: Your own internal experience is the only thing you can always change. Therefore, in order to be successful with this process, it is crucial in Step B that you identify the internal experience you really want. How would you feel if you got your demand satisfied? How would you see yourself if you managed to get what you are demanding? What would you hear inside if your demand were met? *Your answers to these questions will identify your positive intention.* Actually, the fundamental reason you have the addictive demand is in order to experience what you've identified in Step B. You may wish to review Chapter 4 for the fine points of formulating your positive intention.

Your mind always contains the very best solutions to deal with the situations in your life. The challenge you face is to *access this integrated wisdom you already have*. The Choice Process can help you leap over the addictions and core beliefs that roadblock your insight and creativity.

> **THERE ARE ALWAYS WAYS
> TO ACHIEVE YOUR
> POSITIVE INTENTION!**

14 EXPLORATION-INSIGHT PROCESS (EIP)

♥ *The Exploration-Insight Process helps us develop a perspective of the overall picture whenever our minds are running an addictive demand and triggering anger, frustration, fear, or other separating emotions.*

♥ *This integrative process gives us a precise way to explore what is happening inside us in response to a specific incident. Is our response appropriate to the realities of the triggering incident?*

♥ *The EIP helps us put together many pieces of life's jigsaw puzzle so that we can see how our minds are functioning to create our current experiences—and how we may be able to change them in ways we want.*

HOW IT WORKS

The Exploration-Insight Process helps you gain clarity and insight when you are feeling separating emotions. It is a form for organizing and sorting through the life realities and the programming that your rational mind and ego start running when an addictive demand is triggered. It helps you become aware of a number of addictions which then allows you to find the central addictive demand that your separate-self is hung up on. And the EIP offers you a chance to gain new perspectives and insights as you uplevel your addictions into preferences.

You can use the EIP anytime and anywhere—whenever you experience separating emotions. It can be especially helpful with recurring addictive demand patterns that you want more insight about, when you feel tension in your body and want to explore the programming that is producing it, or when you have trouble pinpointing your addictive demands. You can do it silently, aloud, or in writing. You can share it with another person by guiding him/her through it or by having him/her guide you through it.

The EIP can take a minute or two, an hour or two, or anywhere in between. You can spend as much or as little time doing an EIP as you choose; this will depend on how thoroughly you want to explore your programming, the complexity and intensity of your programming, what inner work you have done on it before, and how much time you have to spend on it.

There are six steps in the Exploration-Insight Process. The first four primarily lend themselves to an *exploration* of your separate-self, while the last two give you opportunity to gain *insight* that can help you develop your unified-self programming. Memorize these steps so you can use this process in daily life situations when you need it.

When you are doing an EIP, take each of the steps in turn. Build each step on the previous ones. Any one of the steps by itself can let you have the insight you need to uplevel a demand or let go of it.

EXPLORATION-INSIGHT PROCESS

A. *Incident*
B. *Physical Sensations/Separating Emotions*
C. *What Am I Telling Myself?*
D. *Demand(s)*
E. *Positive Intention(s)*
F. *Living Love Method(s)*

Use present tense words, as if you were right in the midst of the incident. Even if you are recalling an incident from the past, imagine yourself back in the actual situation so you can reexperience your feelings and thoughts. When you do an EIP the moment you feel upset, you can simply observe what is happening as you do each step. If you are going through the EIP aloud, keeping your eyes closed can help you stay in tune with your feelings and with what is going on in your mind. If you're writing, ask yourself the questions, then close your eyes and tune-in to your feelings and thoughts.

Practice using the EIP. Practice doing it aloud. Practice it silently. Practice writing it. You will gain speed, skill, and a sense of when and how an EIP works most effectively for you.

The following step-by-step explanation of the Exploration-Insight Process includes helpful questions to ask yourself and the purpose of each step. Review it often. This information and your own use of the EIP will enable you to become increasingly aware of your addictive programming and, therefore, have greater choice in dealing with it.

EXPLORATION-INSIGHT PROCESS

Here is how you do an EIP:

STEP A: INCIDENT. Using the present tense, specifically pinpoint the exact words or actions that immediately triggered your addiction. Answer the following questions *factually and briefly*: Who is involved? Where is it happening? What is happening? What is being said? Be concise and sensory-based. *Include only what a video camera could record.* Do not include what you think another person is thinking or feeling as part of your sensory-based observation unless you verify your inference by asking him/her if it is correct. In this first step, don't mention your physical or emotional feelings, thoughts, or reactions.

> **PURPOSE:** Our perception is a joint interaction between the observer and that which is observed. We can be aware that sometimes our perception of a life event is accurate—and sometimes we think it's accurate when it is apparent, illusory, or seeming. Webster's Ninth New Collegiate Dictionary describes some pitfalls of perception:
>
> > APPARENT suggests appearance to unaided senses that is not or may not be borne out by more rigorous examination or greater knowledge; ILLUSORY implies a false impression based on deceptive resemblance or faulty observation, or influenced by emotions that prevent a clear view; SEEMING implies a character in the thing observed that gives it the appearance, sometimes through intent, of something else....
>
> The objective, factual description of the situation helps you to see the illusion that is created as your addictive programming interprets that event. It gives you new perspectives and insights. It helps you to experience things as they are without the distortions created by your addictive resisting and clinging.

STEP B: PHYSICAL SENSATIONS/SEPARATING EMOTIONS. When you talk about your physical sensations and emotions, imagine that you are right in that scene. Speak in the present tense. First explore physical feelings: Where do you feel tension or discomfort in your body? Check your head, throat, neck, shoulders, chest, back, stomach, hands, legs. Notice if you feel like crying, the rate and depth of your breathing, the pitch of your voice, your body warmth.

Next: Which emotions are you feeling? (There are lists of separating emotions under the first three centers in Chapter 7.) Get in touch with the specific separating emotions that are involved. They will always be coming from the Security, Sensation, or Power Center, or a combination of these. Don't settle for general terms like "separate," "alienated," "unhappy," or "uncomfortable." Bluntly state your emotions without qualifying them. "I guess I feel" and "a little angry" are ways your ego tries to avoid experiencing or acknowledging what you really feel. "Because" and "the reason is" don't belong in this step.

> **PURPOSE:** This step tunes you in to body tensions and specific separating emotions of your separate-self. It prepares you to become aware of what you are telling yourself. It will help in pinpointing your demand and in using the methods. You simply acknowledge and experience what you are feeling physically and emotionally without defending, judging, or explaining yourself.

STEP C: WHAT AM I TELLING MYSELF? What is your programming telling you that makes you feel the emotions you noted in Step B? How does it want things to be? Additional questions that might be helpful are: What's bothering you the most? What are your models of how things should be or shouldn't be? If things go the way you want, what does it mean about you? If things don't go the way you want, what does that mean about you? What are other people going to think? What is it about you that can't be loved?

Stay in the incident. If you are seeing images, what are they? How do you see the situation? Yourself? The people involved? What expressions do you see on their faces? What else do you see? Explore the feelings that these pictures elicit. What physical sensations and emotions are you feeling? What goes through your head as you experience each of these feelings? Here are some questions that are especially helpful in relation to particular emotions:

> **FEAR:** What's the worst thing that could happen? Imagine that happened: Now what's the worst thing? What is my programming making me avoid? What am I hiding? What is the threat in this situation?

> **GUILT:** Why am I blaming myself? What should I have done? Felt? What would I do if I were completely free in this situation? How do I feel about that?

BOREDOM, FRUSTRATION, OR DISAPPOINTMENT: What do I want to be happening? What would have to be happening so I wouldn't feel bored, etc.?

ANGER: What am I protecting or defending? What would happen if I didn't control? When I can't control, how do I feel about myself, about other people? If the person keeps doing what s/he is doing, what might happen?

Allow yourself to say what comes into your mind, no matter how silly, absurd, wrong, right, unreasonable, untrue, impossible, illogical, irrational, petty, or unfair it seems. Do not censor or limit expressing your addictive programming. Don't try to look good, wise, or "conscious." Don't try to analyze or rationalize away what you are feeling by explaining what you know intellectually to be true. "Well, I know I really don't have to feel this way, and it's kind of silly." Now is the time to acknowledge any separate-self thoughts you've been having that may be keeping you trapped.

Keep the incident in your mind and continue to ask yourself, "Is there anything else I am telling myself that is creating feelings of (anger, fear, jealousy, etc.)?" This step can be given as much time as you wish.

Now step back from your reactions to get a wider perspective on the situation. Ask yourself this question: Are my reactions based on real events, or on guesses or assumptions?*

> **PURPOSE:** To become aware of and consciously express the addictive programming that is triggered by the incident. Also to reassess whether the triggering incident really had the significance that your reaction gave it.

STEP D: DEMAND(S). Now pinpoint your addictive demands: I create the experience of _(separating emotions)_ because my programming demands that _(what you want)_.

List whatever addictive demands seem connected with this matter. Choose the one that is bothering you the most, the one that has the most separating energy behind it. If you don't feel you can select one, you may want to go back and further explore Step C, "What am I telling myself?"

---

* *Taming Your Mind* by Ken Keyes, Jr. can shed some light on the most common pitfalls in clearly perceiving life events. It offers Tools for Thinking that improve the reliability and predictability of our thoughts and ideas. Appendix A has ordering information.

PURPOSE: To formulate your addictive demand(s) that are triggering separating emotions in this incident. This will help you to use the methods in Step F more effectively.

STEP E: POSITIVE INTENTION(S). How would you feel if you actually got that demand satisfied? Or how would you see yourself if things went the way you want? Or what would you hear inside? Now formulate your positive intention:

My positive intention is to see myself as, OR to hear inside that I'm, OR to feel *(internal experience)* .

PURPOSE: To help you get back to an original, underlying, basic motive for running that addictive demand. This can aid you in finding a more skillful way to internally handle the triggering incident.

STEP F: LIVING LOVE METHOD(S). Use one or more of the four methods to work on your demand.

1. The Twelve Pathways
2. Centers of Consciousness
3. Linking Separate-self Emotions with Your Demand
4. Consciousness Focusing

PURPOSE: To use the methods to gain insight so you can handle your addictive demand by upleveling it to a preference, reprogramming it, or taking intellectual responsibility for the separateness you are creating.

AN EIP EXAMPLE

In this example, notice how Sandy precisely follows the six steps and answers the questions that create the Exploration-Insight Process:

STEP A: INCIDENT

Who is involved?
The television repairman and myself.
Where is it happening?
The living room.

What is happening?

I'm looking at the bill he just handed me.

What is being said?

Nothing.

STEP B: PHYSICAL SENSATIONS/SEPARATING EMOTIONS

Where do I feel tension or discomfort in my body?

Tension in my throat, my body has frozen up, tightness in my neck and shoulders, my eyes feel big, constricted shallow breathing, stomach feels like a knot.

Which emotions am I feeling?

Horror, regret, frustration, resentment, anger, indignation, hostility, disappointment, guilt, embarrassment.

STEP C: WHAT AM I TELLING MYSELF?

I'm telling myself that I can't believe what I see! This can't be right—it's way too much. How can those little parts he put in cost so much? Why does everything have to be so expensive these days? I think he's deliberately overcharging me! If our old repairman had done this job, he would've charged much less. I don't like this new company—they're taking advantage.

Sandy, what are you saying? How can you be so sure these people are swindlers? Shame on you for having such thoughts! You shouldn't assume that. What would the repairman think if he knew you suspected his company of taking advantage, after he just spent all afternoon hassling over this set?

Still, I get so irked about these prices! And what am I going to do about this bill? I wasn't counting on such a big one.

What's bothering me the most?

The bill is so high.

What are my models of how things should be or shouldn't be?

The parts shouldn't cost so much. The repairman shouldn't deliberately overcharge me. The old repairman should still be here. The new company shouldn't take advantage. I shouldn't assume the company is taking advantage.

126

How do I see the situation?

The bottom figure on this bill seems to have jumped out and hit me between the eyes.

What images do I have of the other person?

I imagine the repairman as thrusting this bill at me with a smirk on his face, looking like he's ready to let out a big belly laugh like, boy, what a sucker she is for knowing nothing about repairing TVs. He could have put in half a dozen unnecessary parts.

Now I see him as just normally doing his job, not laughing at me, just looking like a regular guy.

How do I see myself?

Suddenly I see myself acting like old Mrs. Smird, complaining about prices being too high and accusing everybody of overcharging.

What else do I see?

There goes the reupholstered chair, the new blender, and repairing the back porch—they all just flew out the window.

What else am I telling myself?

I really resent having to spend so much money on fixing this TV. There are a lot of other ways I'd rather use it.

Are my reactions based on real events, or on guesses or assumptions?

Guesses.

STEP D: DEMAND(S)

I CREATE THE EXPERIENCE OF:	BECAUSE MY PROGRAMMING DEMANDS THAT:
horror	the repairman not give me such a large bill.
regret	I had requested an estimate first.
frustration	the parts not cost so much.
resentment, anger, indignation, hostility	the repairman not deliberately overcharge me.
frustration, disappointment	our old repairman still be here.
guilt	I not assume that the company is swindling me.
embarrassment	the repairman not judge me for thinking he was deliberately overcharging.

The addictive demand that feels the strongest: *I create the experience of horror because my programming demands that the repairman not give me such a large bill.*

STEP E: POSITIVE INTENTION(S)

How would I see myself as, OR what would I hear inside, OR how would I feel if I got that demand satisfied?

My positive intention is to feel peaceful.

STEP F: LIVING LOVE METHOD(S)

I choose to use the Centers of Consciousness Method.

I create the experience of horror because my programming demands that the repairman not give me such a large bill. With this addictive demand, I'm now in the Security Center of Consciousness. I'll play it through the Love Center: (three deep breaths) Physically I feel relaxed. Emotionally I feel calm, peaceful. I sure don't like getting such a big bill from the repairman. But a repairman never knows what he's going to run into or how much needs fixing. Even while I'm questioning whether the bill has to be this high, I'm clear that what I most want is for him to do a good job fixing the TV so we can enjoy watching it. I don't like this situation, and I think I'm getting the message to shop around more for repairs, and to get estimates first. But I can emotionally accept what has happened, and I see this person as a fellow human being who is just playing the role of TV repairman and doing his job the way he thinks it should be done.

CONGRATULATIONS!

You're great to have finished this chapter! The EIP is such a dynamite technique that we have explained it thoroughly. Following the six steps exactly, try it on an incident you feel frustrated or upset about. Then, with that insightful experience, reread this chapter and notice how it "falls into place" in your understanding.

> ## PRACTICE! PRACTICE! PRACTICE!
> ## AND REMEMBER:
> ## THE METHODS WORK—IF YOU DO!

15 WRITTEN EXPLORATION-INSIGHT PROCESS

♥ *Writing out the Exploration-Insight Process can be extremely helpful and insightful.*

♥ *It is especially useful if we're having trouble keeping our minds focused when working alone.*

♥ *Writing out an EIP can give us added perspective and help us recognize that it's all just our programming—and that our programming has nothing to do with who we really are.*

HOW TO DO IT

The next pages present the form for a written EIP. You do not need to answer all of the questions in Steps A through F; yet it may be helpful to read all the questions before you do each step. Any Living Love Method can be used in Step F. You may wish to photocopy the EIP form on the following pages and keep a stockpile handy.

WRITTEN EXPLORATION-INSIGHT PROCESS

STEP A: INCIDENT

Close your eyes and take a deep breath. Focus on an incident in which you felt separating emotions. Perceive the actual situation in your mind. Using the present tense, specifically pinpoint the exact words or actions that immediately triggered your addiction. Answer these questions factually and briefly: *Who is involved? Where is it happening? What is happening? What is being said?* Be concise and sensory-based. Include only what a video camera could record. Do not include what you think another person is thinking or feeling as part of your sensory-based observation unless you verify your inference by asking him/her if it is correct. In this first step, don't mention your physical or emotional feelings, thoughts, or reactions.

_____

_____

_____

STEP B: PHYSICAL SENSATIONS/SEPARATING EMOTIONS

Am I feeling tension or discomfort in my head, throat, neck, shoulders, chest, back, stomach, hands, legs, anywhere in my body? Do I feel like crying? How is my breathing? How does my voice sound? How is my body warmth?

What emotions am I feeling: fear, apprehension, worry, nervousness, anxiety, panic, terror, horror, despair, disappointment, hurt, sadness, helplessness, grief, loneliness, shame, guilt, confusion, embarrassment, envy, doubt, jealousy, frustration, boredom, disgust, anger, annoyance, irritation, impatience, resentment, indignation, hostility, disdain, hate, rage, fury?

_____

_____

_____

_____

_____

STEP C: WHAT AM I TELLING MYSELF?

Write down whatever your separate-self is saying that is making you feel those emotions. *How do I want things to be? What's bothering me the most? What are my models of how things should be or shouldn't be? If things go the way I want, what does it mean about me? If things don't go the way I want, what does that mean about me? What are other people going to think? What is it about me that can't be loved? How do I see the situation? Myself? The people involved? What expressions do I see on their faces? What else do I see? What feelings do these pictures elicit? What physical sensations and emotions am I feeling? What goes through my head as I experience each of these feelings?* We recommend that you consider writing three to ten pages of Step C. This extra concentration involved in writing often helps you draw out some of the programming that's too deep for you to notice by just thinking through this step. Rereading what you've written may help you spot some core beliefs.

_____

_____

_____

_____

_____

_____

_____

_____

_____

What's the worst thing that could happen? Imagine that happened: Now what's the worst thing? What is my programming making me avoid? What am I hiding? What is the threat in this situation? Why am I blaming myself? What should I have done? Felt? What would I do if I were completely free in this situation? How do I feel about that? What am I protecting or defending? What would happen if I didn't control? When I can't control, how do I feel about myself, about other people? If the person keeps doing what s/he is doing, what might happen?

_____

_____

_____

_____

(Go to another sheet if needed.)

Now step back from your reactions to get a wider perspective on the situation. Ask yourself this question: *Are my reactions based on real events, or on guesses or assumptions?*

_____

_____

STEP D: DEMAND(S)

Pinpoint the addictive demands that are triggering the emotions you are feeling. You can use these questions to help you: *What do I really want in this situation? What is it I think I need to be happy? How do I want things to be different? If a magic genie appeared, what one wish would I ask to be granted in this situation? How do I think things should be or shouldn't be, or I should be or shouldn't be? How should I be treated? What would I complain about to my best friend?*

Using the "Pinpointing Addictive Demands" form, formulate whatever demands seem connected with this matter:

I CREATE THE EXPERIENCE OF: **BECAUSE MY PROGRAMMING DEMANDS THAT:**

_____   _____

_____   _____

_____   _____

_____   _____

_____   _____

_____   _____

_____   _____

_____   _____

_____   _____

(Go to another sheet if needed.)

Mark the addictive demand that is creating the strongest separating emotions and work with that demand in Steps E and F.

Photocopy to have on hand when needed.

STEP E: POSITIVE INTENTION(S)

How would I feel if I actually got that demand satisfied? Or how would I see myself if things went the way I want? Or what would I hear inside?

My positive intention is to see myself as, OR to hear inside that I'm, OR to feel

_____.

(internal experience)

STEP F: LIVING LOVE METHODS(S)

Now choose one or more of the four Living Love Methods to uplevel your addiction to a preference. If one doesn't seem to work, try another. Some addictive demands might require you to use all of the methods before you gain the insight necessary to "handle the addiction"—or eventually uplevel the addictive demand to a preference. You may find it helpful to review how to use the method you've selected:

> First Method: The Twelve Pathways. (Chapter 6)
> Second Method: Centers of Consciousness. (Chapter 7)
> Third Method: Linking Separate-self Emotions with Your Demand. (Chapter 8)
> Fourth Method: Consciousness Focusing. (Chapter 9)

Write out how you plan to use one of the methods:

_____

_____

_____

_____

_____

_____

_____

_____

_____

_____

_____

_____

(Go to another page if needed.)

133

YOU'VE DONE IT!

Did you get additional benefits by writing out the Exploration-Insight Process?

♥   ♥   ♥

♥   **WE LOVE YOU**   ♥

♥   ♥   ♥

16

SHARED EXPLORATION-INSIGHT PROCESS

♥   *When a friend is upset, sometimes the most loving and caring thing we can do is to just sit quietly, giving him or her our full attention without giving any advice or suggestions. We're just there while s/he talks about what is troubling him/her—occasionally acknowledging what s/he is saying. And in some situations it can be extremely helpful to guide a person through the Exploration-Insight Process. S/he does not have to understand the process. We can take him/her through the various steps from A through F in a quiet, conversational way.*

♥   *As a friend and listener to someone doing an EIP, we don't give advice, don't diagnose, don't psychoanalyze, don't try to help in any way except by guiding him/her through the process. The game is to use the process to encourage our friend to create his/her own insights in the situation—which can be many times more useful than if we told him/her the same things.*

♥   *There may be times when we want support as we deal with a difficult circumstance. Asking a friend to be present with us as we sort things out, and handing him/her this outline of questions to ask us, can give us wonderful support.*

LEADING A FRIEND THROUGH THE PROCESS

This section is an outline to guide a friend through an Exploration-Insight Process. The person doing the EIP is the speaker, and the person guiding is the listener. The listener guides the speaker by reading each step and then giving the speaker time to respond. Once you become thoroughly familiar with the process, you can ask other "helpful questions," or vary the amount of time spent on any step.

As a listener, the most supportive thing you can do is give the speaker your loving attention and energy while s/he does this process. Advice, insights (aside from the participation indicated), and stories of your own experiences distract the speaker from the inner work s/he is doing.

Get a pen and paper for you to use. Start by sitting and facing one another. Bring your energy together by holding hands, or putting your arms around each other, and breathing deeply in unison six times. Then lead the speaker through the shared EIP.

STEP A: INCIDENT

You say, *Close your eyes and take a deep breath. Focus on an incident in which you felt separating emotions. Perceive the actual situation in your mind. Using the present tense, specifically pinpoint the exact words or actions that immediately triggered your addiction. Be concise and sensory-based. Include only what a video camera could record. Do not include what you think another person is thinking or feeling as part of your sensory-based observation unless you verify your inference by asking him/her if it is correct. In this first step, don't mention your physical or emotional feelings, thoughts, or reactions. Answer these questions factually and briefly: Who is involved?* Give time to answer. *Where is it happening?* Give time to answer. *What is happening?* Give time to answer. *What is being said?* Don't let the speaker ramble or jump to Step B or C. Gently bring the speaker back to only answering the above factual questions.

STEP B: PHYSICAL SENSATIONS/EMOTIONS

You say, *Take a deep breath. Imagine that you are right in this scene. Speak in the present tense. How does your body feel? Are you feeling tension or discomfort in your head, throat, neck, shoulders, chest, back, stomach, hands, legs, anywhere in your body? Do you feel like crying? How is your breathing? How does your voice sound? How is your body warmth?*

If needed, list the emotions you think s/he might be feeling, and say, *Which emotions are you feeling? Fear, apprehension, worry, nervousness, anxiety, panic, terror, horror, despair, disappointment, hurt, sadness, helplessness, grief, loneliness, shame, guilt, confusion, embarrassment, envy, doubt, jealousy, frustration, boredom, disgust, anger, annoyance, irritation, impatience, resentment, indignation, hostility, disdain, hate, rage, fury?*

STEP C: WHAT ARE YOU TELLING YOURSELF?

Using the specific emotion(s) the speaker stated, you say, *What are you telling yourself that makes you feel____?* If appropriate, you might also ask, *How do* you want things to be? What's bothering you the most? What are your models of how things should be or shouldn't be? If things go the way you want, what does it mean about you? If things don't go the way you want, what does that mean about you? What are other people going to think? What is it about you that can't be loved?

Encourage the speaker to get into all the things s/he is telling him/herself. Now is the time to ramble and free associate. It's OK to spend lots of time on this step. *Stay in the incident. If you are seeing images, what are they? How do you see the situation? Yourself? The people involved? What expressions do you see on their faces? What else do you see? Explore the feelings that these pictures elicit. What physical sensations and emotions are you feeling? What goes through your head as you experience each of these feelings?*

What's the worst thing that could happen? Imagine that happened: Now what's the worst thing? What is your programming making you avoid? What are you hiding? What is the threat in this situation? Why are you blaming yourself? What do you think you should have done? Felt? What would you do if you were completely free in this situation? How do you feel about that? What are you protecting or defending? What would happen if you didn't control? When you can't control, how do you feel about yourself, about other people? If the person keeps doing what s/he is doing, what might happen? When the speaker stops, you might ask, *Is there anything else you are telling yourself?*

Now step back from your reactions to get a wider perspective on the situation. Are your reactions based on real events, or on guesses or assumptions? Give time to answer.

STEP D: ADDICTIVE DEMAND(S)

Choosing questions you think might be helpful and giving time between questions, you say, *Pinpoint the addictive demands that are triggering the emotions you are feeling. Use the form: I create the experience of (separating emotions) because my programming demands that (what you want). List whatever addictive demands seem connected with this matter. What do you really want in this situation? What is it you think you need to be happy? How do you want things to be different? If a magic genie appeared, what one wish would you ask to be granted in this situation? How do you think things should be or shouldn't be, or you should be or shouldn't be? How should you be treated? What would you complain about to your best friend?* You write down all the speaker's addictive demands.

You now give this feedback: *I perceive that you are creating the experience of* (your perception of the speaker's separating emotions) *because your programming demands that* (what you think the speaker is demanding).

You say, *Formulate your major addictive demand, the one that is bothering you the most.* It might help the speaker for you to read back the list of demands for him/her to choose from. Write or mark the major demand.

STEP E: POSITIVE INTENTION(S)

You say, *Behind this demand there is a beneficial positive intention. If you were to get this demand satisfied, how would you feel? Or how would you see yourself if things went the way you want? Or what would you hear inside? Use the form: My positive intention is to see myself as, OR to hear inside that I'm, OR to feel (the internal experience you want).* You write down the positive intention using the form.

F. LIVING LOVE METHOD(S)

You say, *Which method would you like to use with this demand to help you achieve your positive intention and to uplevel your addictive demand to a preference?* Depending on the speaker's choice, use one of the following methods:

First Method: The Twelve Pathways. If the speaker chooses this method, you say, *Which way would you like to use this method?* If necessary, list the ways this method can be used:

1. *Say all Twelve Pathways slowly and meditatively, or choose one or more that apply in this situation, and repeat over and over.*
2. *Alternate your addictive demand with one or more or all of the pathways.*
3. *Alternate your positive intention with one or more of the pathways.*
4. *Say your addictive demand, then a pathway, then your positive intention, again a pathway, and repeat this pattern several times.*

Second Method: Centers of Consciousness. If the speaker chooses this method, you say, if necessary, *Which center(s) of consciousness are you using to create your experience of this scene?* and/or, *Imagine and share what it would be like to experience this situation from other centers of consciousness.* Give time for speaker to use Centers of Consciousness aloud.

Third Method: Linking Separate-self Emotions with Your Demand. If the speaker chooses this method, you say, *State your addictive demand using the* *form: I create the experience of (separating emotions) because my programming demands that (what you want).*

You then say, *Using the words from your addictive demand, state your emotional resistance to "what is" in your life. Use the form: I am emotionally resisting*

_____.

You then say, *Realize that in this here-and-now moment "what is" cannot be changed by you in any way. Your suffering is caused by your addictive demand—not by "what is." There are probably other people who are able to enjoy or accept the same situation because they are not emotionally resisting this circumstance. By continuing to emotionally resist "what is" you will only perpetuate your suffering. Explore your suffering. Look at all the ripoffs your addictive demand has been causing you.* If necessary, you turn to Chapter 8 for a list of ripoffs and name the categories aloud. Give time for speaker to list aloud all the ripoffs s/he can think of, and you write them down.

You say, *What payoffs do you think you're getting by holding on to this addictive demand? What do you think you're gaining? What are you afraid you'll lose if you let go? Remember that you're examining the payoffs for holding on to your addictive demand, not payoffs for getting what you want.* If needed, you refer to Chapter 8 for a list of payoffs. Give time for speaker to list the payoffs aloud. You write them down.

You say, *Are you actually getting your demand met by holding on to the addiction? Will holding on to the addictive demand bring inner peace and love into your life? Are these payoffs really worth undergoing the ripoffs you discovered?* Give time for speaker to answer questions.

You say, *Describe the same incident, only this time imagine that you are emotionally accepting "what is." As a preference, what would you see? Hear? Physically feel? Emotionally feel? Taste? Smell? Think? What would be the positive consequences of upleveling the addiction to a preference?* Give time for speaker to describe the incident from a preferential standpoint.

You say, *Now consider how things would be if this addiction were upleveled to a preference. Apply the five characteristics of a preference: (1) You can still want what you want, (2) you can still try to make changes, (3) you can still think you're "right," (4) you can more skillfully achieve your positive intention, and (5) you just don't have to feel upset or unhappy!* Give time for speaker to apply aloud the five characteristics of a preference to his/her incident.

You say, *Choose, for now, to hold on to the addiction or uplevel it to a preference. Either choice is OK.* Give time for speaker to verbalize the choice.

Fourth Method: Consciousness Focusing. If the speaker chooses this method, you say, *Restate your demand and formulate reprogramming phrase(s).* You turn to Chapter 9 for guidelines and beginnings and if needed, suggest phrases. *Which phrase(s) feel(s) best to you?* You write down the phrases.

You say, *Do you wish to use the Affirmative Mode or the Intensive Mode?* If the speaker chooses the Affirmative Mode, you give him/her time to repeat the phrase over and over, either silently or aloud. If s/he chooses the Intensive Mode, allow him/her to get into a reprogramming position. You then say, *Tense your muscles and breathe deeply. Feel all of the suffering that this demand has caused you, time after time in your life. Get in touch with how fed up you are with all the ways this programming has kept you trapped. Use your emotional energy and build your intensity and determination. Begin to say your phrase over and over, first silently and then aloud.* You also get into reprogramming position and reprogram silently or aloud with your partner. Give him/her all the time s/he wants for reprogramming. When s/he seems finished you say, *Keep your eyes closed and review the situation with your new program. Feel the benefits. Appreciate yourself for the freedom you are giving yourself.*

When your friend has completed the EIP, give him/her a hug.

Every time you support someone else doing a shared EIP, you will increase your own understanding as well as your skill in helping people with this powerful tool. Don't let yourself get carried away "trying to help." *Usually less is better.* You are simply providing a framework that will let your friend develop his or her own insights and solutions to life's problems.

Allow quiet spaces to happen during the process. A half minute of silence can often be more productive than quickly jumping into the next step. Give your friend space to do his or her inner work. **On unconscious levels your friend already knows the best things to do to make his or her life work better.** The shared EIP helps your friend bring the wisdom of his or her unconscious mind into conscious awareness. Your job is just to offer a warmly accepting environment that can give your friend an opportunity to make a breakthrough using the Exploration-Insight Process.

GIVING YOURSELF SUPPORT

You may find great value in giving yourself support for your inner work by doing an EIP aloud in the presence of someone you feel comfortable with. His/her presence can help you stay focused on each step until you complete the process. Sharing your work aloud can encourage you to regard your addictive programming as interesting but unneeded baggage which you have been carrying—and are now ready to set down. You also provide a beautiful model for handling addictive stuff as it arises.

> **YOU'RE INCREASINGLY LOVING AND CARING— OUR WORLD NEEDS YOU!**

17 SHARING OF SPACE (SOS)

♥ *When we feel separate from another person, we first use the methods to uplevel our addictive demand(s). We keep doing our inner work until we begin to let go of our separateness.*

♥ *Honoring the Seventh Pathway helps the heart space to stay open and connected: "I open myself genuinely to all people by being willing to fully communicate my deepest feelings, since hiding in any degree keeps me stuck in my illusion of separateness from other people."*

♥ *When we're handling our addictions, we may choose to do an SOS. We ask permission to share with the person we've been feeling separate from. Together, we listen to the programming that was blocking us from achieving our positive intentions. The SOS is for the person sharing it, not the person receiving it. The purpose of the SOS Process is to bring light and healing to a potentially separating encounter.*

A WARNING

There's something we want you to know about the interactive SOS and Conscious Confrontation Processes in the next two chapters. As you get into selecting from the smorgasbord of techniques in this book, a part inside you may resist channeling your thoughts into the detailed forms suggested. This is understandable. We all have a tendency to let our ego-minds follow their own "natural" courses without being aware that our separate-self programming is often getting reinforced. And when it comes to interacting with other people, the increased involvement and *me-vs.-you* habits make it even easier to be lured into the separating games of our egos.

Much of the time people avoid discussing their differences with other people. When they do, notice how they go about it. They try to prove the other person wrong; they try to prove themselves right; they try to teach the other person that s/he shouldn't even be arguing with them! Will against will escalates; personalities clash. Ego-minds quickly jump into security-power-pride struggles of the separate-self.

You may have programming that makes you feel uncomfortable with the next two interactive processes. *Too limiting—too unnatural—too rigid—too confrontational*. Yet people who have persevered with these forms have demonstrated time and time again that they have acquired valuable assets: the ability to communicate effectively in a way that is heard by other people, and more skill in working things out for both themselves and other people. They discover win-win solutions. They like the way their lives work better as they use these processes. And they are sowing seeds for their own personal growth.

Use the forms as crutches until your unified-self has grown strong. After you have used these processes for a year or so, you will find that the forms will fade, and your inner spirit of love and understanding will automatically bloom. *Work to create this benefit for yourself*. You'll know when you've transcended the form and achieved the spirit of cooperation, understanding, empathy, harmony, compassion, and love. Then you can throw away the form—and the essence of the form will automatically be there working for you in your daily life! And it will be there for you when life pitches you the really big ones.

HOW THE SOS WORKS

The Sharing of Space, or the SOS, is a process designed to assist you in openly and honestly sharing the separating feelings you have created in yourself about another person. To keep from using it as a "dump" on another person, first use the Wisdom Principles and Living Love Methods to soften the hardness of any separate-self demands.

Using the SOS Process limits interference from your ego and inspires you to share (1) without blaming and (2) without trying to get the other person to change. It supports you as you break through the walls of separateness you have built around yourself.

On the following page is the form used for the SOS. Begin by acknowledging to the other person that you're wanting to share an SOS. Asking permission invites an openness for a spirit of togetherness to grow.

The second step helps you establish the purpose and framework of your SOS. You are given a choice of saying "awareness" or "intended awareness," depending on whether in the moment you are fully realizing that you have what you need and the other person is indeed a beautiful being. Sometimes you will be sharing from a clear enough space to experience that, and at other times you may still be too caught up in your addictive demand. Use whichever term is appropriate.

Also in Step B you are saying, "…by sharing an illusion I have created." Sometimes you may think that what you are about to share is no illusion—it's a fact! The focus of the illusion is not on any action, but on the distortion in your mind—*your addictive reaction to whatever happened.* Anytime you feel separateness because of an addictive demand, your perception and insight are limited. So in this step you are acknowledging the illusion of your perspective.

> **SHARING OF SPACE (SOS)**
>
> A. Ask, *May I share an SOS with you?*
> B. *Thank you for the gift of listening to my programming. I'm sharing with the awareness/intended awareness that I have everything I need and you are beautiful as you are. I want to feel closer to you by sharing an illusion I have created. I create the experience of __(separating emotions)__ because my programming demands that __(what you want)__.*
> C. *My positive intention is to_____.*
> D. Listen to the other person's response without interruption.
> E. *I hear you say_____.*
> F. *Thank you for being with me.*

After you have spelled out your addictive demand in Step C, share your positive beneficial intention behind that demand. (Refer to Chapter 3 on positive intentions if needed.)

Step D gives the other person an opportunity to respond to the issue you have brought up. You must set aside your thoughts and feelings long enough to clearly hear what the other person is saying. *It is amazing how often people cannot hear what the other person says well enough to accurately feed it back.* This simple step can increase your understanding and cooperation.

In Step E you paraphrase what you heard to the satisfaction of the other person. If s/he interrupts and adds things while you are doing this, simply feed back whatever s/he says without adding any of your own opinions or getting defensive. The point is for the other person to experience being heard. *People like to feel heard!*

Refrain from any further comment, advice, agreement, disagreement, apology, or opinion, except to end the SOS Process with Step F.

GUIDELINES FOR USING THE SOS

1. **USE THE METHODS FIRST:** We strongly suggest that before SOSing, you **use one or more of the Living Love Methods** to (1) uplevel your addictions to preferences or (2) gain what insights you can about the situation. Using the methods before you share helps you take more responsibility for creating your experience. **Regardless of what the other person is doing or has done, you are responsible for creating your own emotional reaction.** The other person is simply "doing what he or she does"—just being himself or herself. S/he is not "doing it to you."

2. **FOLLOW ALL SIX STEPS OF THE SOS:** You'll find that it's risky to change the form. When you do, *your ego will likely get into a back and forth— and start to defend itself.* **The process may soon move from a sharing to a dispute.** Hold to the form and tell your ego to let go!

3. **DON'T DISCUSS THE SOS AFTERWARD:** Don't talk about anything that came up in the SOS Process for at least 12 hours! While you might follow the form exactly and share openly and honestly, if you start talking about it immediately, your ego will probably start trying to prove you're right. The other person may defend and the sharing will then turn into an argument. *It is vital to give you and the other person ample time to do your inner work to gain a greater perspective before you talk about it again.* Hence, 12 hours.

SOS OPTION

Every science develops its own carefully defined terminology. These specially chosen terms point more effectively to nonverbal phenomena than ordinary language usage which usually has several meanings. Imagine how physicists would stumble around if they could no longer use terms such as "mass," "watt," "inertia," "atom," "molecule," etc. As you've noticed, the Science of Happiness uses precision terms that are systematically helpful in making the transition from the separate-self to the unified-self. Our technical terms include *separate-self, unified-self, addiction, preference, programming, positive intention, ripoff, payoff,* etc. While we've chosen everyday words in common use, we have given them a *special meaning* in our context. However, there may be a time when you want to use the SOS Process with someone who is not familiar with the Living Love lingo. Below is a suggestion of how you might translate the SOS into everyday language.

Be sure to follow the three guidelines in the previous section; don't let your ego trick you into starting an argument. The twelve hour integration period afterwards is always helpful.

SOS FORM	**SAME PROCESS— NEW WORDS**
A. May I share an SOS with you?	A. I haven't been feeling comfortable around you lately. I'd like to talk with you about it.
B. Thank you for the gift of listening to my programming. I'm sharing with the awareness/ intended awareness that I have everything I need and you are beautiful as you are. I want to feel closer to you by sharing an illusion I have created. I create the experience of _annoyance_ because my programming demands that _you not chew your gum so noisily._	B. This is just my stuff, and I want you to know what's been going on with me. I'm making myself feel annoyed because I have this thing about gum-chewing. So what I'm wanting is for you not to chew your gum so noisily.
C. My positive intention is to _feel peaceful._	C. My real goal behind wanting that is to feel peaceful inside.
D. Listen to the person's response without interruption. Suppose s/he says, "I didn't realize I was so noisy. You should have told me sooner."	D. Listen to the person's response without interruption. Suppose s/he says, "I didn't realize I was so noisy. You should have told me sooner."

E. I hear you say that _you_
didn't realize you were so noisy, and
I should have told you sooner.

E. I just want to check that I've
heard you correctly. I'm
hearing you say you didn't
realize you were so noisy; that
I should have told you sooner.

F. Thank you for being with me.

F. Thanks for letting me talk
with you about this.

While this example may seem trite or silly, this is the kind of separating stuff
we all refuse to share—or even use the methods with. These are addictions too!
Regular use of the SOS Process will deepen your honesty, your commitment, and
your level of inner work. And remember that even though the person sharing
the above SOS will probably get what s/he wanted (quieter gum-chewing), the
spirit of the process is to share in order *for you* to feel closer by breaking through
an illusion of separateness; it's not to feel closer by getting your addiction satisfied! And there may be times when the other person's response isn't as polite as
in the example. Remember that the only response you're attempting to elicit is
your own inner response of more understanding, less separateness.

When the person you want to do an SOS with is unavailable—or you absolutely will not bring yourself to share with the person you've been feeling separate from—you still have two options. You can have someone else stand in for
that person, and ask him or her to give a response in Step D as if s/he were that
person. Or you can play both yourself and the other person, putting yourself in
the other person's shoes for the Step D response. All of these ways can help you
go beyond the spot of separateness you've been stuck in. Do whatever will help
you get back to loving.

DON'T HOLD BACK

Sharing your separate-self stuff is so important in overcoming it that we suggest you share not just your addictive spaces, but also your thoughts, opinions,
and *all the things you don't want the other person to know!* So much separation can
be overcome in such a short period of time with just regular sharings. If you live
with someone, we think it's especially important to share your "stuff" every day.
Share openly and honestly. Next to doing your inner work, that is one of the
finest gifts you can give another person. Don't hide. There is nothing you have
to hide. The simplest way to realize this is to start sharing all the things you

think you need to hide *as you lean into your unified-self*. Separate-self expression can be separating; *unified-self sharing increases mutual trust and heart-to-heart closeness*. We humans are not as fragile as we might think!

One of the ways your ego may keep you separate from others, and from sharing what you really feel, is having thoughts like, "The other person might get upset," "It'll cause more problems than it solves," and "I'll hurt him/her." That's where you use the Eighth Pathway: *I feel with loving compassion the problems of others without getting caught up emotionally in their predicaments that are offering them messages they need for their growth.* The Eighth Pathway does not insure that the other person will not react to your sharing. If s/he does react, it will be due to his/her own addictive programming—not what you have shared with him/her. No matter what you share, remember: one's addictions are the only immediate, practical cause of separateness and unhappiness.

The SOS Process is not designed to get other people to change. It is designed to get out into the open all the stuff you keep hidden in your head because you tell yourself it's important or real or right or necessary. *It helps you experience just how unimportant it all is.* When you think you must keep your inner thoughts and feelings hidden, you tend to give them an importance that is quite illusory. Hiding a thought or feeling starts a chain of events:

> I hide IT ....
> IT must be important ....
> If IT is important, I must protect IT ....
> To protect IT, I must keep others away ....
> To keep others away, I must hide MYSELF ....
> I wish I knew why I feel so alone ....

When you hide your deepest thoughts and feelings, separation is created in your own heart and mind. *You hurt yourself more than anyone else could hurt you.*

Suppose you're not ready for an SOS. You still want others to change. Then check the Conscious Confrontation Process in the next chapter for its helpfulness in this situation. And remember:

HIDING SEPARATES; OPENNESS UNITES.

**BEING YOU—RIGHT WHERE YOU ARE—
IS A BEAUTIFUL GIFT
TO GIVE ANOTHER PERSON.**

---

18 CONSCIOUS CONFRONTATION PROCESS

♥ *All the principles, methods, and processes we have covered so far are designed to help us love more by demanding less, to help us create inner peace and heart-to-heart love even though "what is" may not be the way we want it.*

♥ *The Conscious Confrontation Process is unique in the Science of Happiness techniques because its purpose is to help us change "what is."*

♥ *The Conscious Confrontation Process is designed to minimize resistance and maximize cooperation when we want someone else to change.*

WHAT IT'S ABOUT

No human being has ever had all of his or her desires satisfied. Every one of us constantly uses our ego-mind to project onto the world ideas or models of how we would like things to be. **And we win some and we lose some.** Many of us try to increase our win-loss ratio through money, prestige, skills, knowledge, careful planning, good looks, sexual attractiveness, and lots of other games. There's nothing wrong with these. Some of them work, more or less, but we are still faced with the naked reality that *no human being ever gets everything that he or she wants in life.*

Most of the people on earth focus most of their efforts on changing the people and situations around them so that they get what they want. Since they are often unsuccessful in changing "what is," they automatically create fear, frustration, anger, hate, resentment, and other separating emotions. When these are experienced fairly continuously, an unhappy life is created.

A wonderful thing about the 2-4-4 system is that it shows us how to play the game of life with both hands: With one hand we try to change the outside world to fit our desires, and with the other we try to change our addictive desires to fit "what is" in the outside world. By flexibly prancing between these two streams of outwardly and inwardly directed energy, we can flow toward a maximum fulfillment of our lives.

As we've pointed out, all the preceding chapters in this book have offered you techniques for increasing your adaptability when "what is" does not meet your models. This chapter will explain *a process that is designed to gently encourage other people to give you what you want.* When it works, you won't have to pay the penalty of creating separateness. Most of the time we use psychological or physical power to push people around in such a way that, when we get what we want, it results in lots of alienation and separateness. *And frequently the long-run disadvantages that this separateness causes us are greater than whatever satisfaction we may experience by getting what we want in the moment.*

As you increase your skill in using the Conscious Confrontation Process, you can often change the outside world and get what you want in life without paying a large penalty in diminished cooperation, love, and inner peace. You do the dance using your unified-self.

> **CONSCIOUS CONFRONTATION PROCESS**
> **(when you want someone to change)**
>
> A. *I make myself feel __(separating emotions)__ when __(briefly indicate situation)__ .*
> B. *I am concerned that what might happen is _____.*
> C. *I would like you to _____.*
> D. *It seems to me that the goal you want is to _____. Is this correct?* Listener nods if goal is correct or indicates correct goal.
> E. *I would like to explore with you some alternatives to help us both achieve our goals. Three ways I have come up with that may be more effective or harmonious are:*
>   *1. _____*
>   *2. _____*
>   *3. _____*
> F. *Thanks for listening to me.*

HOW IT WORKS

Let's look at an example of how the Conscious Confrontation Process can be used. Nancy's husband John sometimes pushes her to have sex when she doesn't want to. Nancy knows that heart-to-heart love is more important than anything else, but she really doesn't like the way John pressures her about having sex and then compares her to an attractive mutual friend when she chooses not to. She wants him to change. She decides to use the Conscious Confrontation Process:

Step A: I make myself feel _angry and resentful_ when _you push me about sex and say I don't want to have sex as often as Betty does with her husband._

Step B: I am concerned that what might happen is _if you keep pushing me I'll develop resistance to having sex, and you'll get more and more dissatisfied and start looking somewhere else for sex._

Step C: I would like you to _stop comparing me with Betty and accept my energy for sex as it is._

Step D: It seems to me that the goal you want is to _enjoy sex with me more often._
Is this correct? (John nods his head vigorously.)

Step E: I would like to explore with you some alternatives to help us both achieve our goals. Three ways I have come up with that may be more effective or harmonious are:
1. _You could take the pressure off both of us by upleveling your addiction for more frequent sex to a preference._
2. _You could express more appreciation to me, and tell me you think I'm attractive. You could be tender with me more of the time whether you want to have sex or not. That might sometimes help me feel more open to sharing sex._
3. _You could show interest in how I'm feeling, and be open to accepting the times and circumstances when I'm not in the mood._

Step F: Thanks for listening to me.

You'll notice that Step A enables you to express how you feel in a situation where there is disagreement. Step B allows you to communicate your concern about what might or might not happen in the future, and Step C requires you to express exactly what you want. These vital elements of person-to-person communication are often missing when we argue with each other—which partly helps to explain why most arguments are fruitless.

In Step D you consider what the other person wants and you ask him/her to validate your inferences. This encourages you to understand the other person's point of view. With Step E you begin searching for possible win-win solutions that will be acceptable to both of you. In this step, be especially aware of any *me-vs.-you* expression in your voice or body language. Try to step out of the situation

151

and perceive it as two wise and fair judges who are working out the best thing to do for two disagreeing parties. Sometimes amazingly simple solutions are waiting to be found that will satisfy both of you. In this step, use your creativity to come up with three alternatives; even if only one of them works, you probably have succeeded in resolving a conflict.

With the single sentence of Step F, you have completed the process. Except for a minimal response to your question in Step D, the other person has been silently listening to you (we hope). When you stop talking after Step F, no doubt your friend will wish to respond. Listen carefully to empathize with what s/he is really trying to say between the lines. Repeat it back asking if you heard him/her correctly. A Harvard study by Borden and Busse revealed that disagreements are best handled when you carefully repeat back what you heard the other person say. This helps the person feel understood, even if you don't agree, and s/he doesn't need to repeat his/her position over and over—meanwhile getting frustrated and hot under the collar.

You'll miss the benefit of the Conscious Confrontation Process if you let an argument develop. It takes two to make an argument! You can't control the other person, but you can make choices for yourself that increase the opportunities for understanding, cooperation, and good feelings. Remember: It's your programming that always creates your emotional experience—not what the other person says or does.

We suggest that you learn to rely on this process. With time and patience it will actually help you get what you want—*when, as, and if a person can give it to you without separateness.* Don't use it as a way to pressure a person or to try to argue him/her into changing. Sometimes the person to whom you have directed this process will need several days to sort out a response. Give him/her plenty of time! Remember that nothing works all the time. That's the way life is. And you can be happy and enjoy your life even when it doesn't meet your models. *That* is the promise of the Science of Happiness.

The love and inner peace you can create and maintain in your heart will bring you far more enjoyment than getting what your programming is making you want. By skillfully using the techniques of the Science of Happiness, you can create the experience of Living Love in your life.

LOVE IS MORE IMPORTANT THAN ANYTHING ELSE!

19 OUR JOURNEY TOGETHER

♥ *From the bottom of our hearts we thank you for reading this book on insight and love. We are on a human journey together. We all want to live in a world in which people are more loving and caring, more personally fulfilled and satisfied with their lives, and more cooperative with each other in creating the great adventure of human life on this planet.*

♥ *We appreciate the part you are playing in helping the people on this earth make the transition from the self-defeating confinement of the separate-self to the life-enriching unified-self.*

♥ *By gathering power through insight and love, you are making your life count in taking steps toward the fulfillment of our human dream together—using our great intellectual and spiritual resources to create human lives characterized by energy, insight, love, happiness, joy, and a feeling of purpose.*

THE CLOCK IS TICKING

Charles Beard, a famous historian, said that one of the great lessons he had found in history was "whom the Gods would destroy, they first make mad with power." In countless ways, the twentieth century has been characterized by our approaching the ultimate in *person-vs.-person* power. Encouraged by technological changes, the unrestrained separate-self ego has run rampant in trapping all of us in a maze of increasing alienation and separateness. In countless ways we've pitted person against person and group against group in struggles that we could not understand and could not go beyond. We've been like bulls pushed into an arena and goaded into *me-vs.-him* fights to the death.

Our species has now divided itself into about 160 separate nations—most of which maintain groups of trained killers and killing machines under the illusion of creating "defense." The financial resources of most of these nations, both large and small, are strained to the utmost to provide the latest missiles, aircraft, warships, guns—all designed to murder fellow humans. With military capability, the egos of our national leaders expand with increasing pride, arrogance, and addictive demands. The real needs for security and peaceful interactions among the five billion people on this earth are brushed aside.

We've experienced the individualistic swamps of "Me first," and "I'm looking out for Number 1," which result in strengthening habits of demanding more and loving less. We've sought to empower ourselves through force and aggressiveness. Since force creates force, our ways have boomeranged on us. The cooperative and loving potential of marriage has often deteriorated into a disparaging battle of separate-self egos. The alienation and paranoia of the separate-self has been constantly stimulated by our divisions into labor and management with its animosities, hatreds, and occasional violence. Our biocomputers in their mad scrambling for *me-vs.-them* power have created a nuclear capacity that has the potential to wipe out all, or almost all, human life on this planet. With the doomsday killing machines we have invented, we have created an ultimate dimension of *us vs. them*. To apply the ancient Chinese saying, if we don't change the direction we're going, we're likely to end up where we're headed!

REARRANGING OUR PRIORITIES

Let us use our technology to change direction to bring nearer the day when the pendulum will begin moving toward cooperation, caring, and a reaching out of heart to heart among all people on earth. Let us replace the *separating power* of brute force with the *unifying power* of insight and love.

It is true, as *Desiderata* says, that "everywhere life is full of heroism." Let us resolve to bring our heroic energy together to build a new world that integrates the wisdom of the heart with the wisdom of the mind. Let us replace the law of force with the force of law. Let us rally all the great unified-self forces so that the twentieth century that is now drawing to a close will be the high water mark of the separate-self. With enough awareness—with the power of insight and love—human-made devastation that is the inevitable curse of the separate-self could progressively be eliminated.

Those of us who have a vision of a higher humanity have a responsibility to lead our fellow humans into our shared birthright: the fulfilling world of the unified-self in which we love and care for others as we love and care for ourselves. One world—living in political, economic, and social cooperation. Let's face it: With the nuclear menace, it's one world—or none.

We hope that you will be so inspired by the attraction of living in a world where people *love more and demand less* that you will resolve to accelerate your journey of personal growth. As planetary citizens, we can add to humanity's chance for survival by using every opportunity to (1) increase our knowledge and **understanding** of the Science of Happiness, (2) increase our **resolve** to acquire these skills so they function automatically in our lives, and (3) to **practice, practice,** and do more **practice** so that our lives are a living demonstration of their beneficial results.

Our adventure in personal growth offers us a greater opportunity for increasing our happiness than anything else we can do. Making the transition from the separate-self to the unified-self is a great and beautiful challenge.

We deeply honor you and appreciate your exploring with us some ways in which we can build together the vision of a new humanity and create the joy of living for everyone on planet earth. We are all so beautiful in our essence. All the horrors and all the dreams we've talked about are just a matter of programming. *And programming is changeable.* A secure, loving, caring humanity is only as far away as our unifying thoughts!

♥ ♥ ♥ ♥ ♥ ♥ ♥

DEDICATE YOUR LIFE
TO THE BIRTH OF THE
NEW HUMANITY

♥ ♥ ♥ ♥ ♥ ♥ ♥

20 ACTION SUMMARY!

♥ *Here's a quick action summary that lets us review the Living Love 2-4-4 system.*

♥ *Whenever we are upset or dealing with a "big problem," we can look over this action summary to increase our effectiveness in handling it.*

♥ *We can use this action summary like a master carpenter who is choosing the best tool to do the job at hand. There are no right or wrong choices—we pick the principle, method, or process that works best for us in each situation we want help with. If one doesn't work, we try another.*

TWO WISDOM PRINCIPLES

1. ADDICTIONS-PREFERENCES
(Chapters 2 and 3)

> **Addictive demands trigger separating emotions that create your unhappiness.**
>
> **Preferences never do.**

A preference is a desire that does not trigger any separating feelings or tensions in your mind or body whether or not your desire is satisfied.

FIVE PREFERENCE CHARACTERISTICS
1. You can still want what you want.
2. You can still try to make changes.
3. You can still think you're "right."
4. You can more skillfully achieve your positive intention.
5. You just don't have to feel upset or unhappy!

PINPOINTING ADDICTIVE DEMANDS
I create the experience of *(separating emotions)* because my programming demands that *(what you want)* .

---

2. POSITIVE INTENTIONS
(Chapter 4)

> **Behind all of our thoughts, feelings, and actions, we always have beneficial positive intentions (even though we may sometimes use unskillful ways to achieve them).**

1. Make your positive intention beneficial, and say what you want, not what you don't want.
2. Make it identify a desired internal state.

INSTANT CONSCIOUSNESS DOUBLER
When you feel separate from yourself or another person:
1. Tune-in to everyone's positive intention.
2. Remember that it's only one person's programming that doesn't like another person's programming.

FORMULATING POSITIVE INTENTIONS
My positive intention is to see myself as, OR to hear inside that I'm, OR to feel:
(internal experience) .

156

FOUR LIVING LOVE METHODS

1. THE TWELVE PATHWAYS
(Chapter 6)

OPTIONS:

1. Say all Twelve Pathways slowly and meditatively, or choose one or more that apply in that situation, and repeat over and over.

2. Alternate your addictive demand with one or more or all of the pathways.

3. Alternate your positive intention with one or more of the pathways.

4. Say your addictive demand, then a pathway, then your positive intention, again a pathway, and repeat this pattern several times.

Memorizing the Twelve Pathways is needed if they are to maximally enrich your life.

2. CENTERS OF CONSCIOUSNESS
(Chapter 7)

SEPARATE-SELF CENTERS

1. Security
2. Sensation
3. Power

UNIFIED-SELF CENTERS

4. Love
5. Cornucopia
6. Conscious-awareness
7. Cosmic Consciousness

USING THE CENTERS

Notice which of the above centers you are using to create your separate-self experience.

OPTIONS:
1. Play the scene in your mind through any other center.

2. Play it through Centers 4, 5, and 6.

3. Play it through all Seven Centers—perhaps with a one-liner.

LOVE EVERYONE UNCONDITIONALLY—
INCLUDING YOURSELF.

3. Linking Separate-self Emotions with Your Demand
(Chapter 8)

1. Pinpoint your **addictive demand** using the form: *I create the experience of ___(separating emotions)___ because my programming demands that ___(what you want)___.*

   Using words from your addictive demand, state your **emotional resistance** to "what is" by finishing this sentence:
   I am emotionally resisting _____.

   Your suffering is caused by your addictive demand—not by "what is." There are probably other people who are able to enjoy or accept the same situation because they are not emotionally resisting this circumstance.

2. Explore the **ripoffs** your addictive demand is causing you.

3. Be aware of the **payoffs** that are tempting you to hold on to this addictive demand. Then actively **question** whether they really exist and are worth undergoing the ripoffs.

4. Consider how things would be with a **preference**. Create detailed, sensory-rich images, sounds, feelings, and thoughts within a preferential framework. Examine the positive consequences of upleveling the addiction to a preference.

5. Check the box that is appropriate for you. *For now, I choose to:*
   ( ) *Hold on to the addiction.*
   ( ) *Uplevel to a preference.*

4. Consciousness Focusing
(Chapter 9)

REPROGRAMMING PHRASE GUIDELINES
1. Phrase is specific; relates to addictive demand.
2. Points to image, thought, or feeling you most want.
3. Feels good.
4. Makes sense to your rational mind.
5. Is pithy, rhythmic, catchy.
6. Has no pressure words like "should" or "will."
7. Has no judgmental words like "bad."

AFFIRMATIVE MODE
Use your reprogramming phrase(s) as you go about your daily activities.

Repeat your reprogramming phrase(s) a total of 1,000 times a day with a counter.

You may choose to run your reprogramming phrase(s) when you are doing intense physical exercise.

INTENSIVE MODE
1. Build up a strong determination to be free of the programming.
2. Be sure you are convinced that it is your programming causing your ripoffs.
3. Develop a ripe realization of what the ripoffs are.
4. Choose reprogramming phrases.
5. On your knees with your face close to the floor, tense your body and begin saying your phrase.
6. Repeat the phrases with strong emotions as long as you feel motivated.
7. Review the same situation with your new program.

FOUR DYNAMIC PROCESSES

1. Choice Process
(Chapter 13)

A. Pinpoint your addiction: *I create the experience of__(separating emotions)__ because my programming demands that ____(what you want)____* .

B. *My positive intention behind this addiction is to see myself as, OR to hear inside that I'm, OR to feel ____(internal experience)____* .

C. *Three new ways to achieve this positive intention are:*
   1. _____
   2. _____
   3. _____

2. Exploration-Insight Process (EIP)
(Chapter 14: The EIP Process)
(Chapter 15: Written EIP)
(Chapter 16: Shared EIP)

A. Incident

B. Physical Sensations/Separating Emotions

C. What Am I Telling Myself?

D. Demand(s)

E. Positive Intention(s)

F. Living Love Method(s)

3. Sharing of Space (SOS)
(Chapter 17)

A. Ask, *May I share an SOS with you?*

B. *Thank you for the gift of listening to my programming. I'm sharing with the awareness/intended awareness that I have everything I need and you are beautiful as you are. I want to feel closer to you by sharing an illusion I have created. I create the experience of __(separating emotions)__ because my programming demands that ____(what you want)____* .

C. *My positive intention is to_____* .

D. Listen to the other person's response without interruption.

E. *I hear you say_____* .

F. *Thank you for being with me.*

4. Conscious Confrontation Process
(Chapter 18)

A. *I make myself feel__(separating emotions)__ when__(briefly indicate situation)__* .

B. *I am concerned that what might happen is _____* .

C. *I would like you to_____* .

D. *It seems to me that the goal you want is to_____. Is this correct?* Listener nods if goal is correct or indicates correct goal.

E. *I would like to explore with you some alternatives to help us both achieve our goals. Three ways I have come up with that may be more effective or harmonious are:*
   1. _____
   2. _____
   3. _____

F. *Thanks for listening to me.*

159

Part 4

APPENDIXES

APPENDIX A

OTHER BOOKS BY KEN

Handbook to Higher Consciousness
Ken Keyes, Jr.
Perfectbound, $4.95

Why are our lives filled with turmoil and worry? Why do we allow ourselves only small dribbles of peace, love, and happiness? The *Handbook to Higher Consciousness* presents practical methods that can help you create happiness and unconditional love in your life. These methods can be used in your everyday life to feel peaceful and secure—despite all the conditions surrounding you. Countless people have experienced a dramatic change in their lives from the time they began applying these effective techniques explained in the *Handbook*. Over three-quarter million copies in print.

A Conscious Person's Guide to Relationships
Ken Keyes, Jr.
Perfectbound, $5.50

If you're looking for effective new ways to give yourself a love-filled, satisfying, wonderful relationship, you will discover them in this book. Here finally is love without tears! This book contains seven guidelines for entering into a relationship, seven for being in one, and seven for decreasing your involvement with gentleness. It describes sound principles that many people have found invaluable in creating a loving relationship.

How to Enjoy Your Life in Spite of It All
Ken Keyes, Jr.
Perfectbound, $5.50

Each one of the Twelve Pathways has an entire chapter devoted to it. These guidelines offer you detailed insights for creating a more enjoyable life. Step by step, you are shown how to take the Pathways from the printed page and make them dynamic tools for bringing increased energy, perceptiveness, love, and inner peace into your moment-to-moment living.

Taming Your Mind
Ken Keyes, Jr.
Clothbound, $7.95

This enjoyable book (which has been in print for 35 years) shows you how to use your mind more effectively. It can enormously improve your success in making sound decisions. It is written in an entertaining style with about 80 full-page drawings by Ted Key, the famous illustrator. It was previously published under the title *How to Develop Your Thinking Ability* and was adopted by two national book clubs. There are over 100,000 copies in print.

Prescriptions for Happiness
Ken Keyes, Jr.
Perfectbound, $3.95

Treat yourself to more happiness by having these three prescriptions handy! They can help you tune-in to your own self-worth—your right to an enriched life—and can help you put more fun and aliveness into your interactions with people. Designed for busy people, this book can be absorbed in a little over an hour. Ideal for gifts.

How to Make Your Life Work or Why Aren't You Happy?
Ken Keyes, Jr. and Tolly Burkan
Perfectbound, $3.95

In an entertaining way, Ken offers this timely message for people who want to improve the way their lives are working. It is simple for a beginner, yet deep enough to offer insights to all. You'll enjoy the succinct style and cartoons on every other page! Can be read in less than an hour. Many folks feel as though it had been written expressly for them.

Your Heart's Desire—A Loving Relationship
Ken Keyes, Jr.
Perfectbound, $3.95

Do you want to bring the magic of enduring love into your relationship? All of us have had a taste of what heart-to-heart love is like. We cherish those times and strive to experience them continuously. Using your rich inner resources, this book can help you to create a more loving relationship—without your partner having to change! It offers support for you to beautifully deepen the harmony, love, empathy, and trust you now enjoy.

The Hundredth Monkey
Ken Keyes, Jr.
Pocketbook, $2.00

There is no cure for nuclear war—ONLY PREVENTION! This book points out the unacceptability of nuclear weapons for human survival. It challenges you to take a new look at your priorities. With the intriguing concept about the power of our combined efforts, it shows how you can dispel old myths and create a new vision to save humanity.

APPENDIX B

WORKSHOPS FOR PERSONAL GROWTH

The Ken Keyes College in Coos Bay, Oregon offers a variety of personal growth workshops. Depending on your needs and interests, some are as short as a weekend, many are five-day courses, and some are longer. All of the trainings are designed to show you how to break through your personal roadblocks to enjoy your life more fully. The emphasis is on the practical application of the Science of Happiness in your daily life—instead of knowledge alone.

The Science of Happiness focuses on things you can do to increase insight, love, energy, and the joy of living. The lives of over 20,000 students, housewives, businessmen, teachers, counselors, doctors, and others have been enriched by the workshops we have been giving since 1972. People are discovering that the Science of Happiness presents methods that work—regardless of the "up-and-down" circumstances in their lives.

The workshops cover such topics as relationships, parenting, career, communication skills, relating in business, money, body and health, and opening our loving spirit. These high-quality courses include room, board, and instruction at nonprofit prices that run about one-half the usual cost of other workshops. Many people come for one training and stay for several. All of the life-expanding trainings give the participants opportunities to discover more about themselves and to grow in ways that help them live more effective lives.

Besides helping you define who you are, you will be encouraged with specific ways to accept and appreciate yourself and others more. Once you have learned to use these methods, you will be able to devote yourself to a deeper level of inner work that will heighten your satisfaction in life and improve your interactions with others.

Coos Bay is a beautiful city located on scenic U. S. 101 along the Oregon coast. It has the third largest harbor on the west coast of the United States, and there are many attractive beaches nearby. Across the street from the College are public tennis courts, jogging trails, and a delightful duck pond. Within an hour's drive, there are spectacular waterfalls and the Oregon Dunes National Recreation Area. Coos Bay is easily accessible by car, bus, or air.

TO GET A CATALOG

For a free catalog of workshops and other courses offered by the College, send your name and address to Registrar, Ken Keyes College, 790 Commercial Avenue, Coos Bay, OR 97420. Without charge you will receive a quarterly catalog listing nonprofit workshops, books, audiotapes, and videotapes. If you wish more information about the trainings, you may phone the registrar at (503) 267-6412.

THE KEN KEYES COLLEGE
COOS BAY, OREGON

loving more

Living Love

demanding less